Pages of the Qur'an
The Lygo Collection

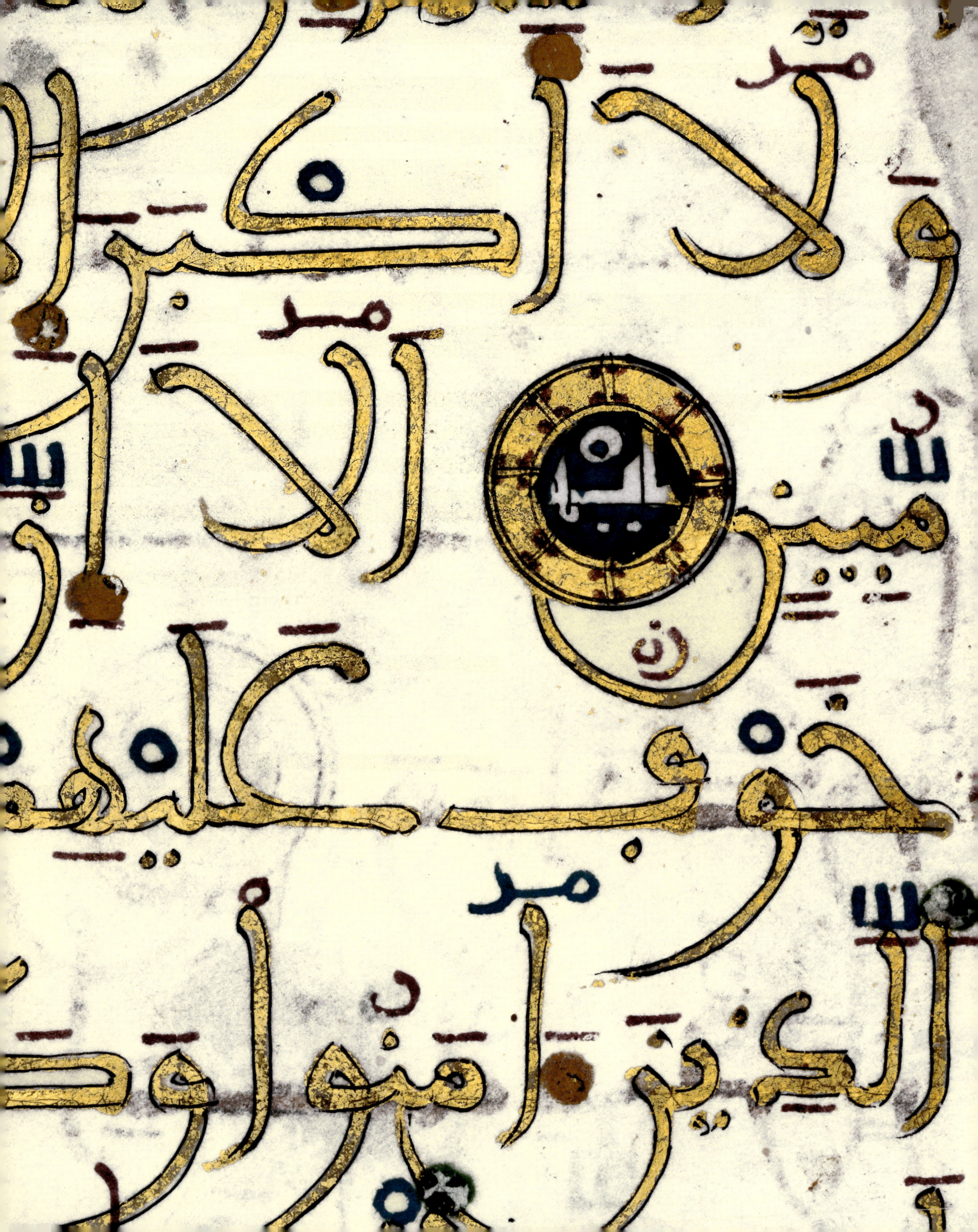

Pages of the Qur'an
The Lygo Collection

Will Kwiatkowski

Paul Holberton publishing, London

Produced by Paul Holberton publishing
89 Borough High Street
London SE1 1NL
www.paul-holberton.net

in association with

Sam Fogg, Ltd.
15D Clifford Street
London W1S 4JZ
www.samfogg.com

ISBN 978-0-9553393-5-6
All rights reserved

British Library Cataloguing in Publication Data
A catalogue record for this book is available from the British Library

Photography by David Brunetti

Design and colour correction by
Anikst Design, London

Printed by E-graphic, Verona, Italy

Acknowledgments
Some of the descriptions in this catalogue are condensed versions of entries written by Marcus Fraser for the catalogue accompanying the exhibition *Ink and Gold: Islamic Calligraphy* held in the Museum für Islamische Kunst, Berlin, in 2006. Use was also made of some of the descriptions for the exhibition *The Illuminated Word: The Qur'an 650–1930* at Sam Fogg, London, 2008. The help of Misha Anikst, Manijeh Bayani, Katie Boycott, David Brunetti, Marcus Fraser, Charlie Schriwer and David James was invaluable in producing this catalogue.

Contents

Introduction 6

Catalogue 10

Bibliography 130

Introduction

The Lygo Collection consists of over seventy leaves and bifolia from Qur'an manuscripts written between around a century after the Prophet Muhammad's death in 632 CE and the middle of the sixteenth century. They include pages from some of the most celebrated manuscripts of the period as well as lesser-known ones, and provide a comprehensive overview of stylistic developments in Qur'anic calligraphy and illumination. During the period represented, Islam became the religion of the majority in the Near East and North Africa and spread to parts of Central Asia, the Indian subcontinent and sub-Saharan Africa. At the same time, the scripts and formats used for copying and illuminating the Holy Word multiplied and developed. Trade, war, diplomacy and the search for patronage ensured the constant movement of artisans, manuscripts and traditions, though regional variations of script and illumination in areas such as the Maghrib were remarkably tenacious.

The consistent esteem in which the art of the calligrapher was held across the Islamic world reflected the status of the Qur'an as the unmediated word of Allah and its centrality to notions of Islamic culture and identity. Though the Arabic language and script have a long pre-Islamic history, Arabic blossomed as the dominant spoken, literary and administrative language of a civilization following the expansion of Islam in the seventh and eighth centuries. In the early Islamic period there quickly emerged a variety of cursive scripts used for administrative purposes and epigraphic scripts used on monuments and luxury objects. This division was not absolute, and there were scripts that combined elements of both types. The earliest Qur'ans, for example, were written in an essentially cursive style frequently referred to as 'Hijazi' that incorporated many elements of epigraphic scripts (Gruendler 1993, pp. 131–39).

The format and even aspects of the orthography of these early Qur'ans were rooted in the late Antique and especially Syriac manuscript tradition (George 2010, pp. 40–42). In the Umayyad period, however, Qur'an production took distinctly new aesthetic directions. In the scripts that are misleadingly though near-universally known as 'Kufic' after the city of Kufa in Iraq, the proportions of the letter forms and the dimensions of the text block and page were laid out according to geometric principles. Though this aesthetic may have had roots in classical notions of harmonious proportions, its application to script was entirely new (*ibid.*, pp. 56–60, 95–108). Qur'ans in Kufic script also quickly abandoned the vertical format of late Antique and Hijazi manuscripts in favour of a horizontal one. This enabled the extensive use of *mashq*, the horizontal stretching of the letter forms that is a stylistic feature typical of many Kufic scripts (e.g. nos. 1, 3, 11, 15, 18, 20, 27).

Though Kufic scripts came to be associated largely with copies of the Qur'an, their development has been linked to the challenge of reproducing sections of Qur'anic and other texts on highly symbolic buildings such as the Dome of the Rock in Jerusalem and on important monuments such as milestones (*ibid*., pp. 60–71). A key role has been assigned to the Umayyad Caliph 'Abd al-Malik, who commissioned the building of the Dome of the Rock, and in whose reign many of the early milestones were erected. Significantly, 'Abd al-Malik also made the hitherto bilingual Greek-Arabic administration entirely Arabic, and replaced all iconography on the coinage with purely epigraphic designs.

Different types of Kufic scripts were produced in different periods and concurrently and over a wide geographical area. Some Kufic scripts seem to have been used largely for copies of the Qur'an with a large number of lines of text per page (e.g. nos. 3, 9, 10, 26, 27), while others were used for small copies with relatively few (e.g. nos. 31–34). The most expensive leaves were elaborately illuminated with devices marking chapter, verse and other textual divisions (e.g. nos. 6, 15), while others were left with almost no decoration (e.g. nos. 5, 16). Luxury copies were also sometimes copied in gold, an expensive and laborious process that required the copying of the entire text in a glue base before the application of the gold and the outlining of the letters in a dark ink (nos. 10, 21, 30). Precise origins for manuscripts have been difficult to establish owing to lack of colophon information, though certain features such as the use of the letter *sad* for sixty in the *abjad* system, and other orthographic features, have been associated with the Western Islamic lands (nos. 14, 19, 23, 26, 29, 35).

By the tenth century a new type of angular Kufic script, characterized by contrasting thin and thick ligatures and certain cursive features, was being used to copy the Qur'an (nos. 41, 43, 44, 46, 47, 49, 50, 52). This type of script, known as 'New Style' or more commonly but misleadingly as 'Eastern Kufic' script, was related to cursive scripts that had been used for administrative papyri and non-Qur'anic texts as early as the seventh century (Déroche 1992, p. 132). At around the same time, scribes also started to use the purely cursive *naskh* script that had also developed in the administration. The earliest dated Qur'an in *naskh* script is a famous single-volume copy on paper in upright format by the scribe Ibn al-Bawwab, completed in Baghdad in 391 / 1001 (Rice 1955).

The concurrent adoption of paper and an upright format for many copies of the Qur'an with cursive scripts can also be linked to bureaucratic practices. The 'Abbasid bureaucracy in Baghdad was quick to replace papyrus with paper, and Baghdad became a flourishing centre of paper-making (Bloom 2001, pp. 47–50).

The acceptance of changes in script and format in the more conservative sphere of Qur'an production may well be linked to the emergence in this period of a mass-Muslim society in which the Qur'an would have been read by private individuals. In these kind of non-institutional settings, and particularly in regions where Arabic was not the native language, legibility and standardization would have been important concerns. These concerns could also account for the concurrent development of the standard systems of orthography and vocalization (e.g. nos. 48, 49, 52) that are still in use today. Cost may also have been a factor in the acceptance of these changes. Paper was far cheaper and more widely available than parchment and cursive scripts were also quicker and therefore cheaper for copying the Qur'an. Many manuscripts in the new scripts were also textually dense with a high word count to the page, which might also indicate commercial rather than institutional or imperial production (e.g. nos. 46, 49, 50).

Of course, grand, multi-volume Qur'ans in elaborate versions of the new scripts on expensive, high-quality paper were also made after the gradual acceptance of these changes (e.g. no. 47). In North Africa and Spain paper never displaced parchment as the primary material for copies of the Qur'an in the medieval period. Probably the most famous Qur'an from the Western Islamic lands, the so-called 'Nurse's Qur'an', completed in Qayrawan in 410 / 1019–20, was copied in a giant, highly distinctive variant of Eastern Kufic script on parchment (no. 44). Around the same time, a distinct type of cursive script dubbed 'Maghribi' began to be used for both secular and Qur'anic manuscripts in Spain and North Africa (nos. 45, 53–57).

Interestingly, at the same time that new scripts were being used for the copying of the Qur'an, these scripts were subjected to the same kind of rules of proportion that had been applied to Kufic scripts. These proportions were based on the rhombic dot formed by the nib of the pen and circles using the height of the letter *alif* as the diameter (George 2010, pp. 108–14; 132–34). A key role in this process is traditionally assigned to Ibn Muqlah (886–940), who acted as vizier to a succession of 'Abbasid caliphs in Baghdad in the first half of the tenth century, and is said to have chosen six cursive scripts, subjecting them to these proportional principles. Ibn Muqlah's system is said to have been refined by Ibn al-Bawwab, and subsequently by a third master, Yaqut al-Must'asimi (d. 1298), who worked at the court of the last 'Abbasid caliph, al-Musta'sim (d. 1258), and subsequently for the chief vizier of the Mongol Empire, 'Ala al-Din 'Ata Malik Juwayni, after the termination of the 'Abbasid Caliphate.

Yaqut is said to have had six famous students, including the calligrapher Arghun al-Kamili, who was responsible for five copies of the Qur'an in beautiful *rayhani* script (no. 62). Another of Yaqut's pupils, Ahmad ibn al-Suhrawardi, was responsible for at least one of a series of magnificent, monumental Qur'ans made for the Mongol Emperor Öljeïtu (r. 1301–16) in the early fourteenth century (James 1988, chaps. 4, 5). As with

Ilkhanid architecture, the monumentality and expense of these Qur'ans reflected the scale of the Chingizid dynasty's global empire, stretching from China to Iraq and Russia, and its claims to universal dominion.

The Mongols were matched in monumental Qur'an production by their political rivals, the Mamluk dynasties who ruled Egypt and parts of Syria between 1250 and 1517. The transfer of both artisans and actual manuscripts from the Ilkhanid to the Mamluk domains has been established (O'Kane 1996; James 1988, pp. 103–10) and it has been suggested that monumentality in Mamluk architecture and manuscript production was an artistic response to the Mongol challenge, or even an assertion of Mamluk confidence after the collapse of the Ilkhanid Empire in the 1330s (Fraser and Kwiatkowski 2006, p. 102). Timur, the founder of the Timurid empire in Iran and Central Asia, saw himself as a successor to Chingiz Khan and the restorer of the Mongols' world empire, and monumentality continued to be a feature of architecture and manuscript production under his patronage and that of his descendants. In the Mongol, Mamluk and Timurid empires, *muhaqqaq* was the script usually used for large-scale Qur'ans (nos. 60, 61, 63, 64, 67, 68, 70) probably on account of the stately flow of the sublinear parts of the letters. *Naskh*, on the other hand, continued to be used for small-scale copies (e.g. no. 59).

The latest leaves from the Lygo Collection (nos. 72, 73) date from the beginning of the period in which the art of the master calligrapher witnessed a partial disassociation from Qur'an and manuscript production in Iran and Central Asia. This process was concomitant with the rise in popularity of collections of individual paintings and calligraphic specimens in poetic and epistolary scripts, often signed by master artists, in the form of albums. Large, luxury copies of the Qur'an continued to be copied and illuminated in Safavid Iran, however, even though the Qur'anic text was not the primary vehicle for the master calligrapher's art (no. 73). These were most frequently in *naskh* or *muhaqqaq* script, but also in combinations of these and other scripts. In the Ottoman Empire the art of the calligrapher continued to be associated to a closer degree with the copying of the Holy Word, and master calligraphers like Şeyh Hamdullah (d. 1520) and Ahmed Karahisarı (d. 1566) were celebrated for their copies of the Qur'an as well as for *kit'a*, individual calligraphic panels of pious inspiration meant for inclusion in albums.

1
Monumental leaf in Kufic script
Near East or North Africa
8th century CE
Surah 22 (*al-Hajj*), vv. 26–31

Folio from an Arabic manuscript on parchment, twelve lines of brown Kufic script per page; individual verse divisions marked with vertical row of fine diagonal lines

55.7 × 64.5 cm

This leaf comes from a monumental Qur'an approximately one third of which is today located in Tashkent. The manuscript was in Istanbul in the late fifteenth century when it was presented as a gift to the Naqshbandi Sufi order. It was then placed by the famous Sufi Shaykh Khwaja 'Ubaydallah Ahrar (d. 1490) in the mosque-*madrasah* that bears his name in Samarkand (Paris 2007, p. 106). The manuscript was in St Petersburg by the late nineteenth century, when it is thought that many of the folios now in Western collections became detached. It was examined there by the orientalist A.F. Shebunin (Shebunin 1891) and a facsimile of it was published in 1905 (Uspenskij and Pisarev 1905).

The manuscript is one of the largest known Qur'ans to have been produced on parchment and belongs to a group of manuscripts of similar size and script, fragments of which are in Paris, Cairo, Sana'a, Damascus and Gotha. Though tradition frequently associates this Qur'an and others in the group to the Caliph 'Uthman (d. 656), today they are largely attributed on the basis of the script to the eighth century CE (see von Bothmer 1997, p. 105; Déroche 1999, p. 65; Déroche and von Gladiss 1999, no. 5; Paris 2001, no. 14). Carbon tests of a folio from the same manuscript as this leaf showed a 68% probability of a date between 640 and 765 and a 95% probability of a date between 595 and 855 (see Christie's, 22 October 1992, lots 225, 226).

Further leaves from the same manuscript are in the Aga Khan Museum (Paris 2007, no. 33) and the Nasser D. Khalili Collection (London 2004, no. 1). Another leaf appeared at Sotheby's, 9 April 2008, lot 1.

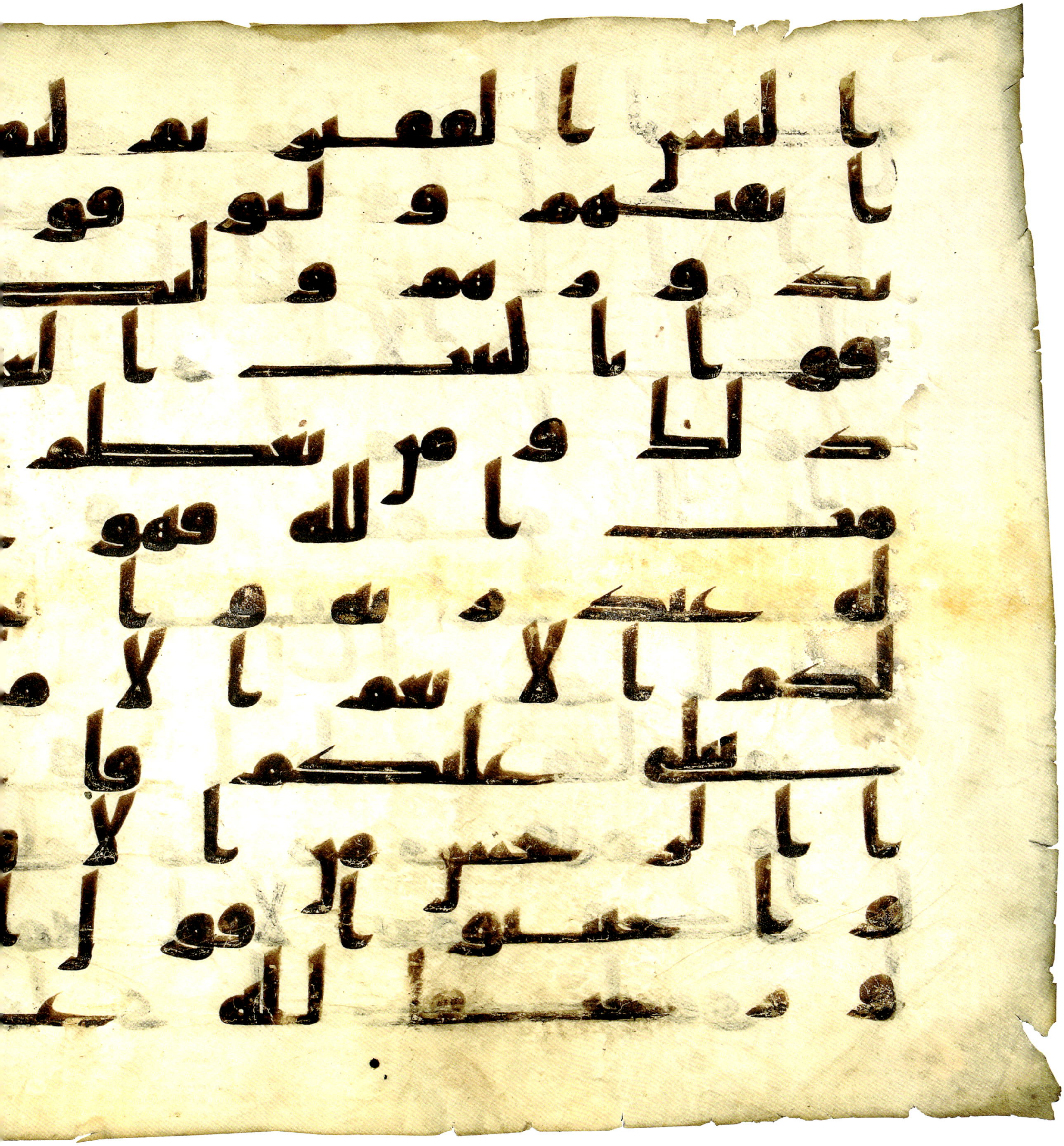

2
Leaf in Kufic script
Near East or North Africa
8th century CE
Surah 49 (*al-Hujurat*), v. 15 – Surah 50 (*Qaf*), v. 14

Folio from an Arabic manuscript on parchment, sixteen lines of dark brown Kufic script per page; vocalization in form of red dots; *surah* heading in gold; tenth verse marker in the shape of illuminated gold and polychrome rosette

19.3 × 26 cm

This leaf displays interesting features associated with early Kufic scripts and manuscript illumination. Since the mid 1970s several leaves and sections from this dispersed Qur'an have been published, allowing a wide survey of its style. A number of aspects of the stylized script are typical of the Umayyad period: there is almost no use of letter pointing (*'ijam*), which appears only on the terminal *nun*, and the vocalization, in the form of red dots, is undeveloped. There is a distinct archaism to certain letter-forms, most noticeably in the terminal *qaf* and occasionally in the terminal *ya*, which droop in a hook-shape below the line. The script is similar, although not identical, to style B.II in François Déroche's classification of 'Abbasid scripts (Déroche 1992, pp. 38–39).

Leaves from the same manuscript are found, among other collections, in the Musée du Bardo, Tunis (Paris 1982, no. 344); the Cincinnati Art Museum (Welch 1979, no. 5); and the Freer Gallery of Art, Smithsonian Institution, Washington D.C. Others have been sold at Sotheby's, 6 April 2011, lot 3; 13 April 2000, lot 1; and 23 April 1997, lot 39; and at Christie's, 23 May 1986, lot 78.

بسم الله الرحمن الرحيم

3
Leaf in Kufic script
Near East or North Africa
8th century CE
Surah 4 (*al-Nisa'*), vv. 123–30

Folio from an Arabic manuscript on parchment, sixteen lines of dark brown Kufic script per page; later letter-pointing in form of brown ink dashes; vocalization in form of red and green dots; single verse divisions are marked with a short row of three diagonal brown ink dashes; fifth verse divisions are marked with a slightly larger letter *alif* drawn with a thin nib in brown ink and infilled with decoration in brown and green; the ink on the verso, which is the hair side, has worn and been re-inked at a later date

32.4 × 39.1 cm

This folio comes from a widely dispersed manuscript of the Qur'an that is notable for its singular script and for several archaic features. The script is characterized by a strong degree of horizontal stretching (*mashq*), a very rounded form to the terminal *nun*, which visually punctuates the page, and a relatively tightly spaced layout, both in terms of the number of words and letters per line and in terms of the number of lines per page. There are other idiosyncrasies of the script, such as the distinctive medial *fa/qaf* and *'ayn* that sit above the line of script, attached by a very thin ligature to the base line. All these have led François Déroche to assign the manuscript a script category all of its own, group F (see Déroche 1992, pp. 46–47).

Déroche has linked the style to two inscriptions of the eighth century, one dated 100 / 718–19, the other dated 160 / 776–77 (Déroche 1992, p. 42). Marcus Fraser has also linked the extended tail of the form of the letters *'ayn* and *ghayn* to two manuscripts dated *c*. 700 and *c*. 710–15 (Fraser and Kwiatkowski 2006, p. 27).

Other features suggesting an early date are the original lack of letter-pointing, single verse divisions in the form of three angled dashes – a feature found on Hijazi and

early Kufic material (see nos. 1, 4, 5, and Déroche 1992, p. 21) – and *surah* titles, not present here but visible on other published folios, with the title in red Kufic squeezed in above or below a panel of green, brown and red illumination. Marcus Fraser has shown how *surah* titles of this type predate the later variety in which gold and the title of the *surah* itself are prominent features of the illumination (Fraser and Kwiatkowski 2006, pp. 27–28).

An unusual feature is the use of a large letter *alif* drawn in brown ink and internally segmented in brown and green for the fifth verse markers. The most common device in Kufic Qur'ans for marking fifth verses was a Kufic letter *ha* in gold, representing the number five in the *abjad* system. In other early Qur'ans different markers are found, however. In the famous Tashkent Qur'an (see no. 1), which has been dated *c.* 700, the fifth verse markers appear as small devices of circular or square format decorated predominantly in red, green and brown.

4
Leaf in Kufic script
Hijaz, Yemen or Egypt
8th century CE, vocalization added 10th century
Surah 88 (*al-Ghashiyyah*), v. 22 – Surah 89 (*al-Fajr*), v. 30

Folio from an Arabic manuscript on parchment, fourteen lines of brown Kufic script per page; restricted letter-pointing with two angled dashes to differentiate the letter *ta*; vocalization in form of red and green dots, occasional red *shaddah* symbols, further vocalization in green; original single verse divisions marked with vertical rows of two or three dashes, later additions in red and green; fifth verses marked with small *ha*-shaped motifs and the word *madaniyan* in small brown Kufic script; tenth verse divisions marked with square or rounded knot-motifs outlined in brown ink decorated in red, green and brown-yellow; *surah* heading drawn in brown ink with vegetal and geometric internal motifs, blank central panel, lower panel filled with an inscription enumerating verse, word and letter counts of the *surah*, majority of heading panel coloured in red, green and brown-yellow

20.5 × 32.7 cm

The erratic script of the present leaf, containing elements associated with both Hijazi and Kufic scripts, probably places the leaf in the late seventh or first decades of the eighth century CE, a stage of calligraphic development between the Hijazi and fully formed Kufic script.

The original design of the *surah* heading, with a long lateral panel extending across the page and a stepped increase in height at the left end, is of an archaic type generally accepted as dating from the Umayyad period. Several other folios with related but even more primitive forms of *surah* heading panel containing text in archaic script are in the Topkapi Saray Library in Istanbul (inv. no. 194), the Bibliothèque nationale, Paris (or. arabe 334) and in Sana'a, Yemen (Dar al-Makhtutat, inv. no. 00-28.1).

We can tell from the verse count of Surah 89 (*al-Fajr*) on this folio that the original verse numbering was organized according to a Hijazi tradition. Though this does not give us a firm geographical origin, the Hijazi tradition (whether Meccan or one of the two Medinan traditions) was most often used in the early centuries of Islam in the Hijaz, Yemen and Egypt. The nature of the script, the archaic *surah* heading, and the use of the Hijazi numbering combine to suggest a date of 720–50.

The coloured vocalization, the vertical rows of coloured dots marking verse divisions, the stylized *ha*-shaped motifs marking fifth verse divisions, and the inscriptions in small brown script were added by a Qur'anic scholar or scribe at a later point, probably in the tenth century. The inscription squeezed into the lowest tier of the *surah* heading gives the verse count according to the two Medinan, Basran and Kufic traditions. The word *madaniyan*, referring to the two Medinan traditions, also appears alongside the fifth verse divisions. Though these various traditions developed in the eighth century, they were not classified until the late ninth century. The scribe has also used the system of vocalization associated with Khalil b. Ahmad al-Farahidi (d. 786), which does not seem to have come into common use until the tenth century. The *surah* heading, which would originally have been in simple brown ink, was probably coloured at the same time that the later annotations were added.

5
Leaf in Kufic script
Near East or North Africa
8th century CE
Surah 8 *(al-Anfal)*, vv. 52–72

Folio from an Arabic manuscript on parchment, seventeen lines of brown Kufic script per page; occasional later additions of letter-pointing in a grey ink; individual verse divisions marked with vertical row of angled dashes in brown ink; tenth verse divisions marked with simple red circles

13.5 × 18.6 cm

The script on this Qur'an leaf is closest to group B.Ib in François Déroche's classification of early scripts. Déroche has compared the scripts on manuscripts in this style to inscriptions such as that on the al-Ta'if dam, dated 58 / 677–78 (Déroche 1992, pp. 35–36). Another indication of an early date are the faint *surah* markers in the form of a row of angled dashes, a feature found on Hijazi and early Kufic leaves (see nos. 1, 3, 4, and Déroche 1992, p. 21). The poor linear discipline, while a feature of early leaves in general, is extreme here to the point that it also probably suggests a provincial origin.

Some of the text was strengthened at a later date in a darker ink.

6
Leaf in Kufic script
Near East or North Africa
8th or early 9th century CE
Surah 81 *(al-Takwir)*, v. 11 – Surah 82 *(al-Infitar)*, v. 8

Folio from an Arabic manuscript on parchment, seventeen lines of dark brown Kufic script per page; vocalization in form of red dots; single verse divisions marked with triangular clusters of six gold dots; tenth verse divisions marked with a rectangular motif containing a stylized inscription with the verse number; *surah* headings consist of title and verse count in gold Kufic around a long rectangular knotted design with remnants of a gold palmette in the margins

20 × 26 cm

The *surah* heading on this leaf would seem to represent a transitionary stage between Umayyad *surah* dividers in the form of decorated bands and mature 'Abbasid manuscripts in which the *surah* title itself, written in gold, constituted the main element of the *surah* heading. Interestingly, the name and verse count of the concluding *surah* (*al-Takwir*) is given above the panel, as well as those of the *surah* beginning below. *Surah* headings on other leaves from the same manuscript (see Christie's, 7 April 2011, lots 1, 2) vary in the use of decoration and headings, further indicating that the Qur'an was illuminated in a period of experimentation.

The script most closely resembles group B.II in François Déroche's categorization of 'Abbasid scripts (Déroche 1992, pp. 35–36, 39). This is most clearly visible in the forms of the independent *nun*, the final *qaf*, and the initial *ha*. The longer lower return of the independent *alif*, however, looks forward to more mature 'Abbasid scripts in Déroche's group D (Déroche 1992, pp. 43–45).

The script, dimensions, illumination and the variety of different formats for the *surah* headings are closely related to those on a Qur'an once housed in Meknes (see no. 7).

A section of the same Qur'an is in Bibliothèque royale, Rabat (Paris 1999, no. 139).

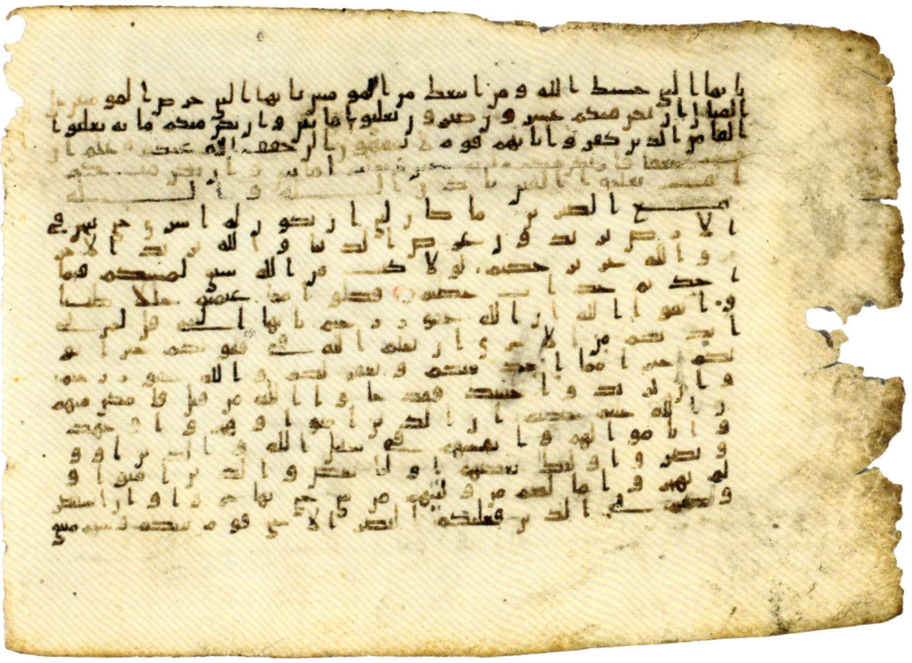

5

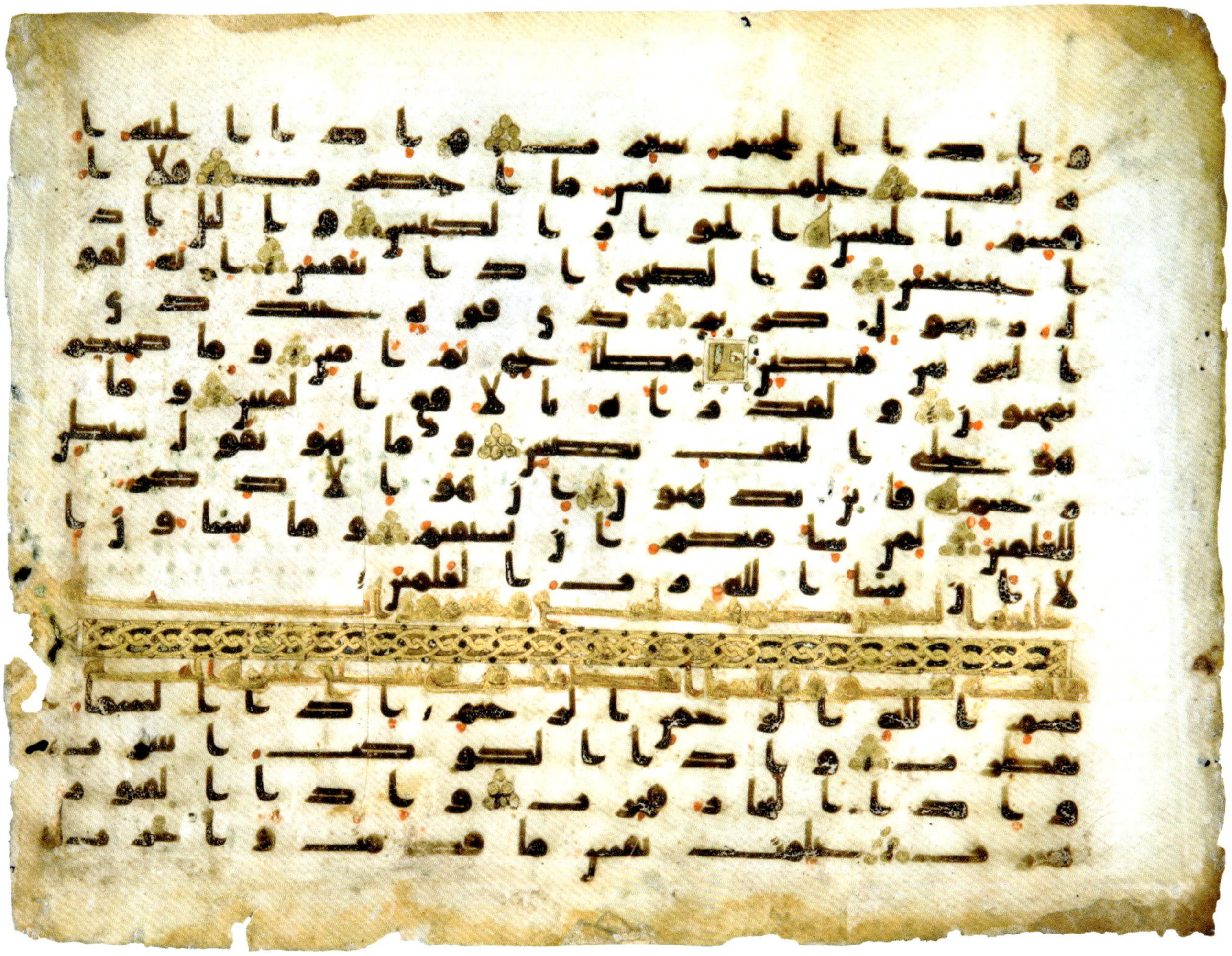

6

7
Leaf in Kufic script
Near East or North Africa
2nd half 8th century CE
Surah 2 (al-Baqarah), vv. 14–26

Folio from an Arabic manuscript on parchment, seventeen lines of brown Kufic script per page; vocalization in form of red dots; individual verses marked with triangular clusters of gold dots; fifth verse division marked with gold letter *ha*; tenth verse division marked with rectangular illuminated device

18.5 × 27.4 cm

This leaf comes from a manuscript that was once housed in the city of Meknes in Morocco, the bulk of which is now housed in the Tareq Rajab Museum, Kuwait. The German scholar and traveller Gotthelf Bergsträsser (1886–1933) visited Meknes in the late 1920s and took photographs of the nearly complete codex, then in the possession of a certain Sherif 'Abd al-Rahman Zidan. The present folio was among the leaves recorded by Bergsträsser, whose photographs are held in the Corpus Coranicum at the Berlin-Brandenburg Academy of Sciences and Humanities.

The script is very similar to that of no. 6 and shows the same basic affinity to Déroche's group B.II, along with tendencies towards the more mature 'Abbasid scripts. The verse divisions are also marked with the same illuminated features as those on no. 6.

A leaf from this manuscript was sold at Bonhams, 15 April 2010, lot 3.

8
Leaf in Kufic script
Near East or North Africa
2nd half 8th century CE
Surah 58 (al-Mujadilah), vv. 1–8

Folio from an Arabic manuscript on parchment, sixteen lines of brown Kufic script per page; vocalization in form of red dots; *surah* heading in form of gold band with repeated geometric pattern on recto side; losses to text areas and with some repairs

19.5 × 25 cm

The script on this leaf places the manuscript to which it belonged in a small group copied in a style that marked a transitional phase between the early Hijazi script and the Kufic scripts of the 'Abbasid period. Scripts belonging to this group, classified as B.Ia by François Déroche, are essentially Kufic in form, but retain features of the Hijazi style, notably the rightward slope of the vertical upstrokes (see Déroche 1992, p. 35). Another feature of this group, visible here, is the slight upward curve of the tail of the final form of the letter *mim* (Déroche 1992, p. 39).

The type of geometric decoration on the band dividing the *surahs* is characteristic of manuscripts of the period, though it has been illuminated with gold rather than in the more typical plain brown ink (see Déroche 1992, nos. 7–8).

7

8

9
Leaf in Kufic script
Near East or North Africa
8th century CE
Surah 25 (*al-Furqan*), vv. 53–70

Folio from an Arabic manuscript on parchment, seventeen lines of brown Kufic script per page; vocalization marked with red dots; occasional letter-pointing; occasional verse markers in red or green, otherwise left blank

18.6 × 25.3 cm

The script on this leaf falls into the category of distinctive scripts classified as group C by François Déroche (Déroche 1992, pp. 36, 40–41). The final form of the letter *nun,* which is written in a single sweep ending in a triangular flourish, is reminiscent of group C.II (Déroche 1992, pp. 40–41). The return of the *alif* is generally longer than that typical in manuscripts in this group, though it is not flattened as is the case with group C.III. The shortened tail of the final *mim* is more typical of manuscripts in the C.III group.

For another leaf from this manuscript, see Stanley 1995, no. 1.

قصد نا مس ا وم الك
السماء خلفه لمر
لكن اسود سمى وعاد
اخى طمه عمل وا
د لايهم فلما و
مستفر وا مقا ما ل
ال قو و اما و كا د رس
ال ها اخ ا للعمر ف
هل ك الا لما ظ لم
ا ر ا و اقلبه و حدك و هما
لك الذ ر ا سيا يهم حسا و كا

10
Leaf in gold Kufic script
Near East or North Africa
Late 8th or early 9th century CE
Surah 38 (*Sad*), vv. 36–60

Folio from an Arabic manuscript on parchment, fifteen lines of gold Kufic script outlined in pale brown ink per page; letter-pointing in pale brown ink, later letter-pointing in dark ink; vocalization in form of red and blue dots; individual verses marked with a diagonal row of gold dashes outlined in brown; fifth verse divisions marked with a stylized letter *ha* in gold Kufic script within a gold roundel; tenth verse divisions marked with an illuminated square device containing an *abjad* letter giving the exact verse count; text area surrounded by a band of plait motifs drawn in brown ink and illuminated in gold, red, green and blue on reserved ground, the corners and mid-points of the bands having square knot motifs in gold; a stylized vegetal motif extends into the margin from the mid-point of the outer band

27.4 × 36.8 cm

This folio is from the second volume of a famous Qur'an written entirely in gold script, every page of which is framed by an illuminated border. The entirety of the first volume and most of the second volume are in the Nourosmaniye Library in Istanbul, while individual leaves from the second volume are found in major collections in Europe and the United States.

Only a handful of Qur'ans were written in gold Kufic script. The manuscript from which this folio comes and the famous Blue Qur'an (see no. 27), which is of similar dimensions, are by far the largest of the group. These manuscripts are of great richness and luxury, and must have been an extremely costly undertaking.

The technique of chrysography (writing in gold) differs from that of ordinary calligraphy in brown ink. Instead of dipping the nib of the stylus into ink and drawing it across the page to form the letters, the chrysographer first wrote the text in a liquid glue. Next the gold was applied on to the glue, automatically assuming the basic calligraphic form of the glue 'script'. As this would have left the script with a slight lack of definition and clarity, the letters were outlined in brown ink.

26

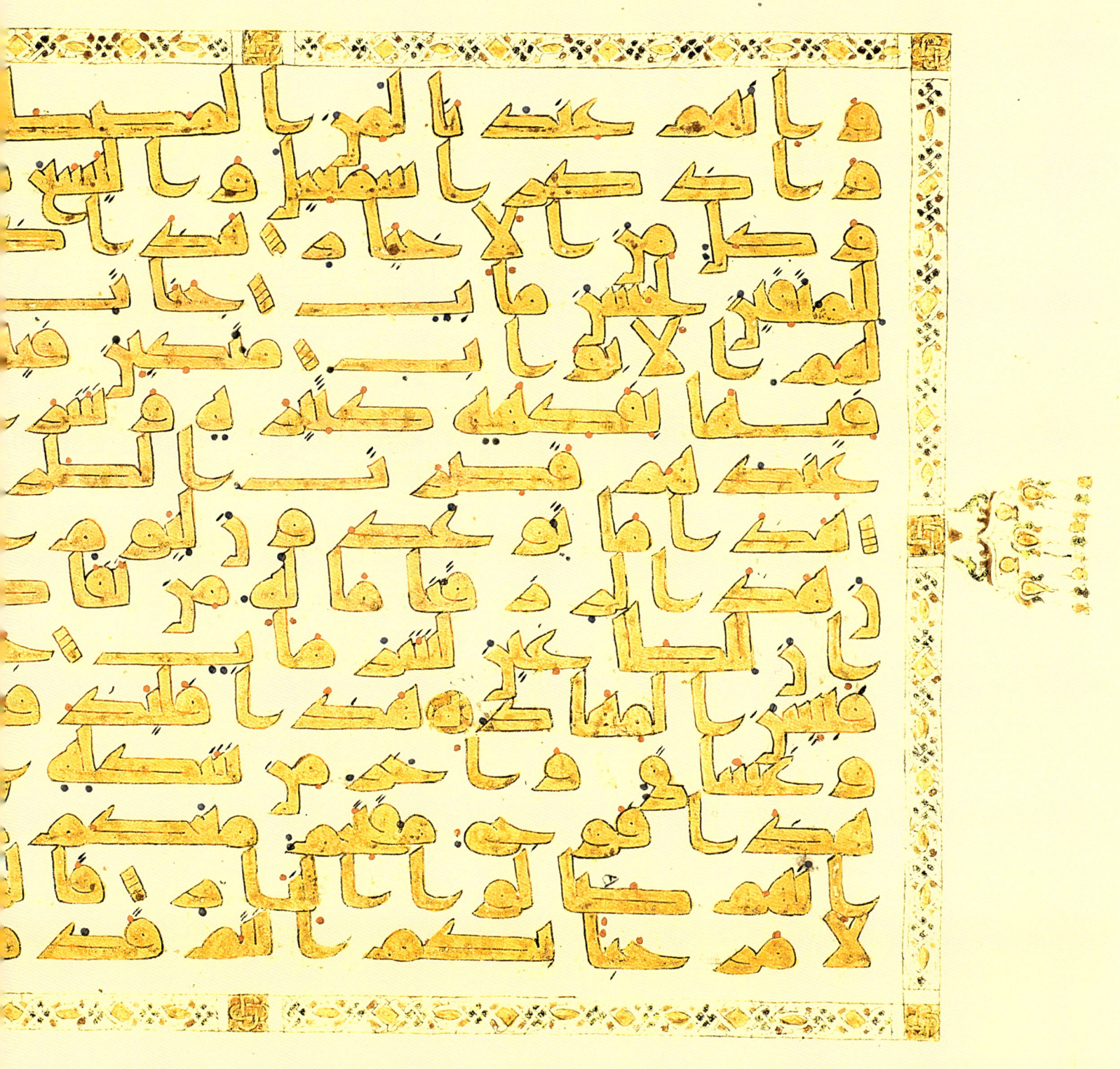

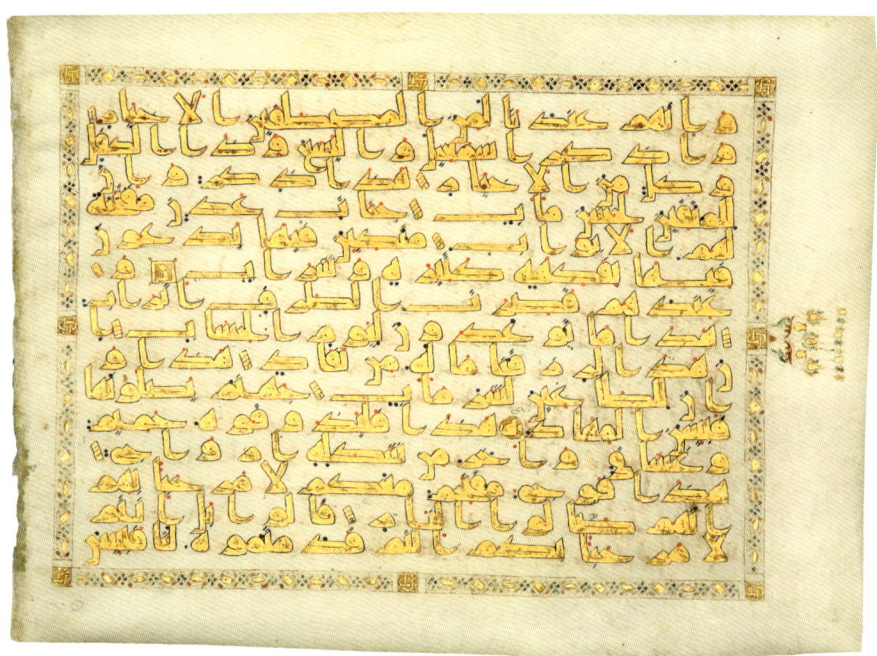

Cat. 10 reverse

There was an early Islamic precedent for the writing of the Holy Word in gold. The tenth-century scholar Ibn al-Nadim, author of the *Kitab al-Fihrist*, tells us that in the early eighth century the scribe Khalid b. Abi'l-Hayyaj copied a gold Qur'an for the Umayyad caliph 'Umar b. 'Abd al-'Aziz (r. 717–20 CE), who had been inspired by the gold inscription on the mosque in Medina. The caliph is said to have shown his appreciation for the manuscript, but found the requested price too high and returned it to the scribe (Dodge 1970, p. 11; Stanley 1995, p. 7).

Though the script has been classified as type D.IV in Déroche's categorization (Déroche 1992, pp. 44–45, 90), many letter forms are closer to type D.I. Whereas most of the Qur'ans in the D category have been attributed to the ninth century, there are indications that this manuscript can be ascribed to the eighth or at least the early ninth century. These include the use of a diagonal row of dashes to mark verse divisions, a feature found on early Qur'anic manuscripts including those in Hijazi script (see nos. 1, 3, 4, 5, and Déroche 1992, p. 21). The use of a continuous border band surrounding the text on every page is also a feature associated with early Qur'ans. Though border bands framing pages where *juz'* or *surah* divisions fell was a feature of Kufic Qur'ans from the eighth through the tenth centuries, there is only one other published manuscript with a border band on every page. This is a fragmentary codex discovered in the Sana'a Mosque cache, dated by von Bothmer to the eighth century (von Bothmer 1987).

Single leaves or bifolia from the manuscript from which this leaf derives are to be found in various collections including those of the Cleveland Museum of Art, the David Collection, Copenhagen, and the Nasser D. Khalili Collection (for the latter two examples see von Folsach 2001, p. 55; Déroche 1992, no. 41). The five folios in the Khalili Collection were on show in the exhibition *Heaven on Earth: Art from Islamic Lands* at the Courtauld Institute in 2004 (London 2004, no. 2). Another folio from the manuscript was exhibited in the Museum für Islamische Kunst, Berlin, in 2006 (Fraser and Kwiatkowski, no. 5).

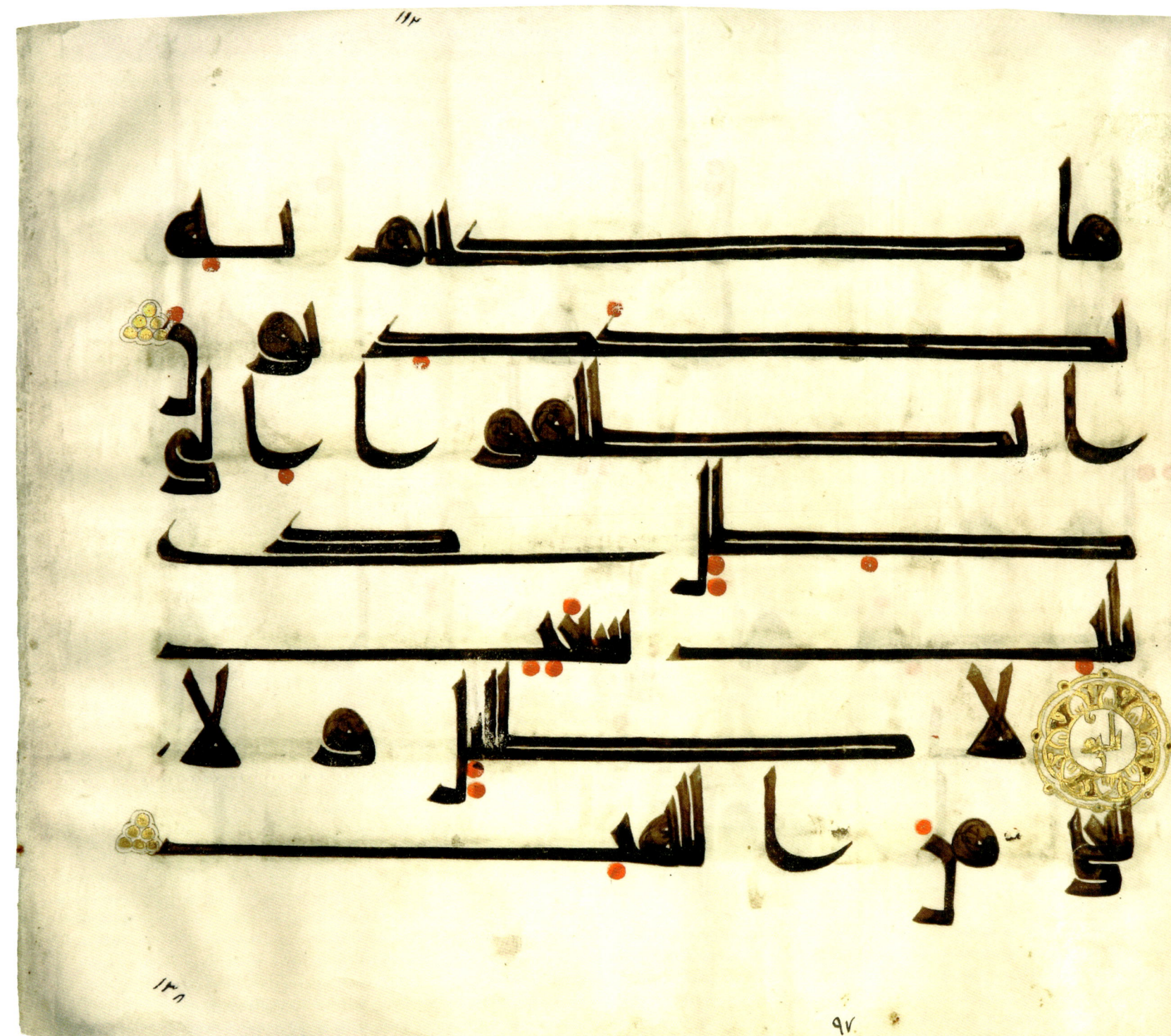

11
Leaf in Kufic script
Near East or North Africa
9th century CE
Surah 77 (*al-Mursalat*), vv. 26–31

Folio from an Arabic manuscript on parchment, seven lines of dark brown Kufic script per page; vocalization in form of red dots; verse markers in form of triangular clusters of six gold dots; tenth verse marker in gold rosette inscribed with the word *thalathun* (thirty)

23 × 32 cm

This pristine leaf on beautiful white parchment comes from a famous manuscript made in the Near East or North Africa at the very height of luxury 'Abbasid Qur'an production. Aesthetic considerations clearly overshadowed functional ones: horizontal stretching of the beautifully proportioned letter forms is taken to an extreme, and there is no letter-pointing to aid reading of the text. The script is closest to the style classified by François Déroche as D.I, which was used for some of the most aesthetically refined manuscripts of the period, such as the famous Qur'an donated by the governor Amajur to a mosque in Tyre in 875–76 CE.

A section from this Qur'an in the Iran Bastan Museum, Tehran, inv. no. 4289, is illustrated in Lings 1976, no. 5. Another leaf from the same Qur'an is in the Chester Beatty Library, Dublin, published in James 1980, no. 5. James lists other pages as belonging to the Boston Museum of Fine Arts and the Pars Museum, Shiraz. A leaf from this manuscript was exhibited in the Museum für Islamische Kunst, Berlin, in 2006 (Fraser and Kwiatkowski 2006, no. 8).

بسم الله الرحمن الرحيم

12
Leaf in Kufic script
Near East or North Africa
9th century CE
Surah 5 (*al-Ma'idah*), vv. 94–101

Leaf from an Arabic manuscript on parchment, fourteen lines of black Kufic script per page; vocalization in form of red dots; *hamzat al-qat'* marked with yellow dot; individual verses marked with triangular clusters of three gold dots outlined in black; tenth verse division marked with gold rosette containing the verse count in *abjad*

24.4 × 33.5 cm

This leaf has some of the characteristics of group F in François Déroche's classification of 'Abbasid scripts, most noticeably the strongly curved final and independent *nun* and thick trumpet-like flourishes to the ends of the letters *nun*, *waw* and *lam*. The distinctive medial forms of the *qaf/fa* and *'ayn/ghayn* that characterize manuscripts in this script (see. no. 3) are not visible here, however, where these forms of the letters resemble more those in the D group. Other features, such as a forked ending to some of the letters, and the final forms of the letters *qaf* and *ya*, the hooks of which drop to the line below, are characteristic of group C. This mixture of styles and the illumination, which is typical of manuscripts in mature 'Abbasid scripts (e.g. nos. 11, 22), suggest an origin in the ninth century CE.

A further interesting feature of the script are the thin, spike-like extensions to some of the final letter forms. This feature is also found in nos. 26, 29 and 35, which, like this leaf, show a mixture of features from groups C and D.

A section and several individual folios all from the same manuscript have appeared at Sotheby's, 6 April 2011, lots 167, 171, 173, 174; and 6 October 2010, lots 1, 2.

13
Leaf in Kufic script
Near East or North Africa
9th century CE
Surah 64 (*al-Taghabun*), vv. 2–16

Folio from an Arabic manuscript on parchment, sixteen lines of brown Kufic script per page set in a later gold, green and red frame; later letter-pointing in form of black dots; *shaddah* and *sukun* added later in green ink; verse markers indicated by gold *ha*-shaped devices; tenth verse markers indicated by large illuminated decorated roundels

16 × 25 cm

The later gold, green and red frame surrounding the text of this Qur'an leaf, probably added in the Ottoman period, suggests that it was once part of an album or used as a *levha,* a framed calligraphic inscription. The script is closest to category D.IV according to François Deroche's classification of 'Abbasid scripts (Déroche 1992, pp. 37, 43–45). This script seems largely to have been used for Qur'ans with a high number of lines to the page. Two leaves in a similar script, also transformed into album pages, are in the Nasser D. Khalili Collection (Déroche 1992, pp. 36, 37). Unusually, there are neither coloured dots for vocalization nor original letter-pointing.

14
Leaf in Kufic script
North Africa or Western Mediterranean
9th century CE
Surah 11 (*Hud*), vv. 43–53

Folio from an Arabic manuscript on parchment, twelve lines of brown Kufic ink per page; vocalization in form of red dots; letter-pointing in dark brown ink; yellow and green dots mark *hamzat al-qat'* and *hamzat al-wasl*; *shaddah* marked with semi-circle in red ink; long alif marked with red line; fifth verse divisions marked with three *ha* letters in colours and gold

18 × 25 cm

An interesting feature of this folio are the unusual marks along the vertical side of the text area. Perhaps used as a method of ruling, they are not commonly seen in Qur'ans of this period (Déroche 1992, p. 123). Another unusual and striking feature is the complex fifth verse marker in the form of three consecutive *ha* letters in red, green and gold.

The scribe has used hemicircles as *shaddah* symbols and a vertical stroke to mark unwritten *alifs*. These are practices that have been associated with the Maghrib and the Western Mediterranean (Blair 2006, p. 122; see also nos. 23, 26, 29, 35).

A leaf from the same Qur'an is in the Nasser D. Khalili Collection (Déroche 1992, no. 68), and a further example was sold at Bonhams, 8 October 2009, lot 6.

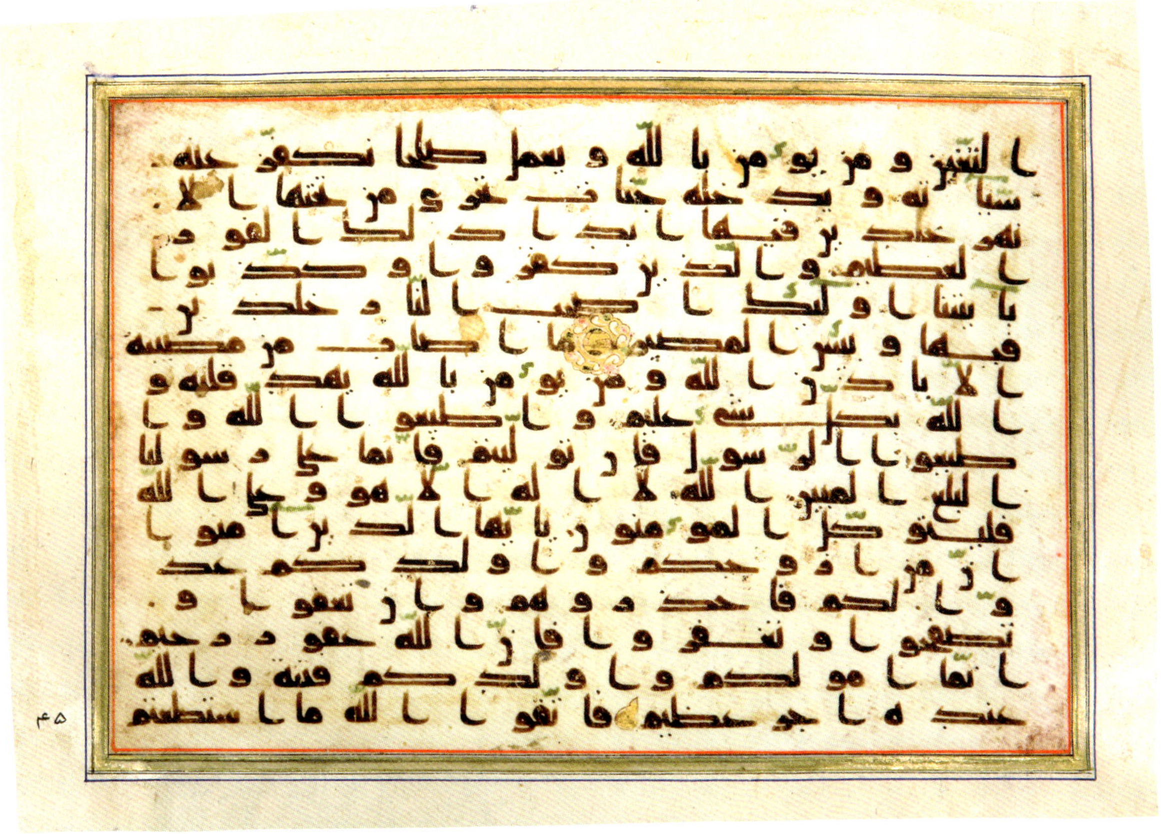

13

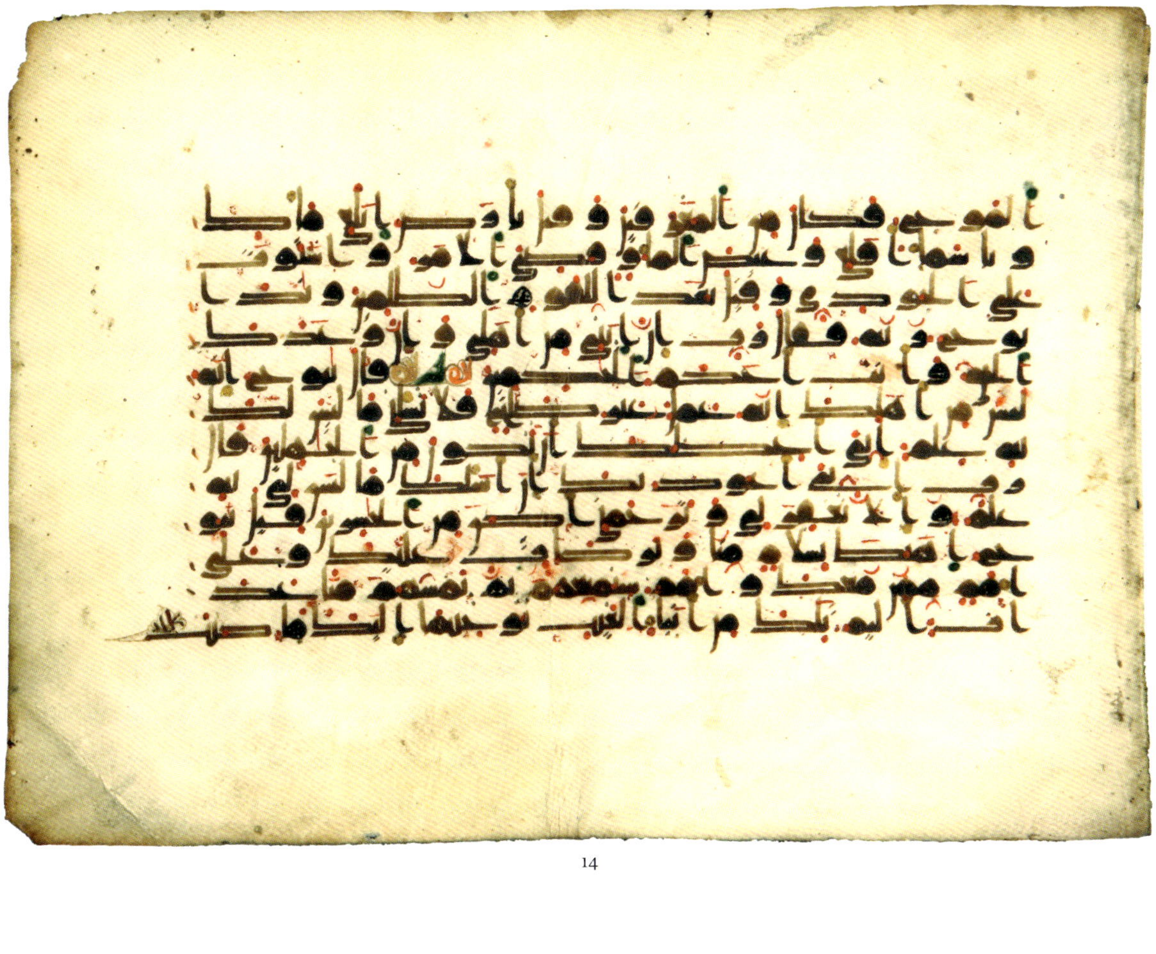

14

15
Leaf in Kufic script
Near East or North Africa
9th century CE
Surah 94 (*al-Sharh*), v. 8 – Surah 95 (*al-Tin*), v. 6

Folio from an Arabic manuscript on parchment, seven lines of brown Kufic script per page; later interlinear comments in a later Arabic hand; vocalization in form of red dots; single verse divisions marked with triangular clusters of six gold dots; fifth verse division marked by the letter *ha* in gold; *surah* heading consists of title and verse count in gold ornamental Kufic on a floral background set in a rectangular panel with plaited border, with a large gold medallion extending into the margin

22.8 × 32.4 cm

This luxuriously illuminated leaf comes from the same manuscript as no. 11. The beautifully preserved *surah* heading contains the title (*al-Tin*) and verse count (eight), ending in a palmette formed of a delicate gold vegetal pattern, filled with tiny black, green and red dots. For a contemporary illuminated *surah* heading that incorporates a similar double-leaf pattern, see a leaf in the Nationalbibliothek, Vienna (Duda 1992, fig. 17).

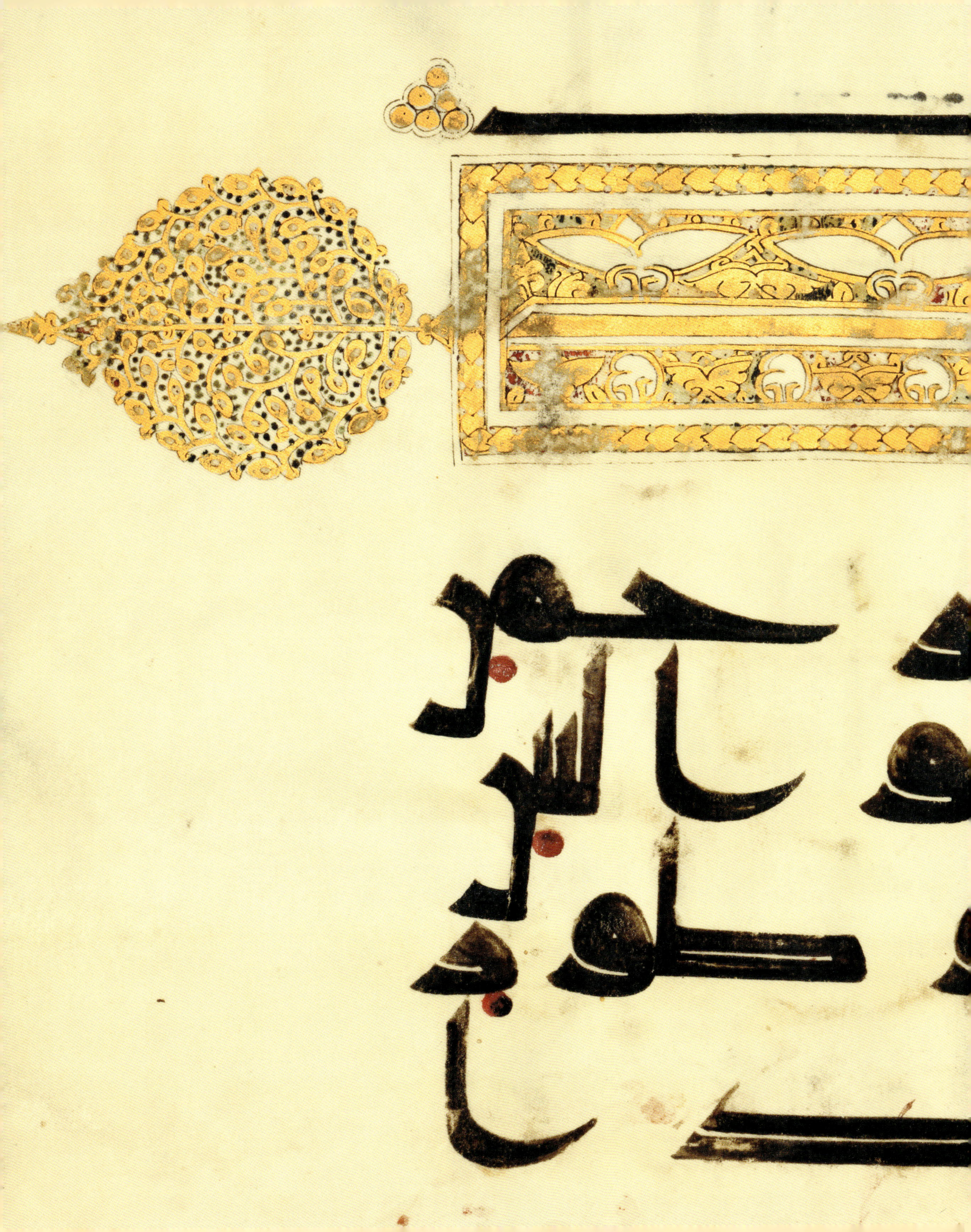

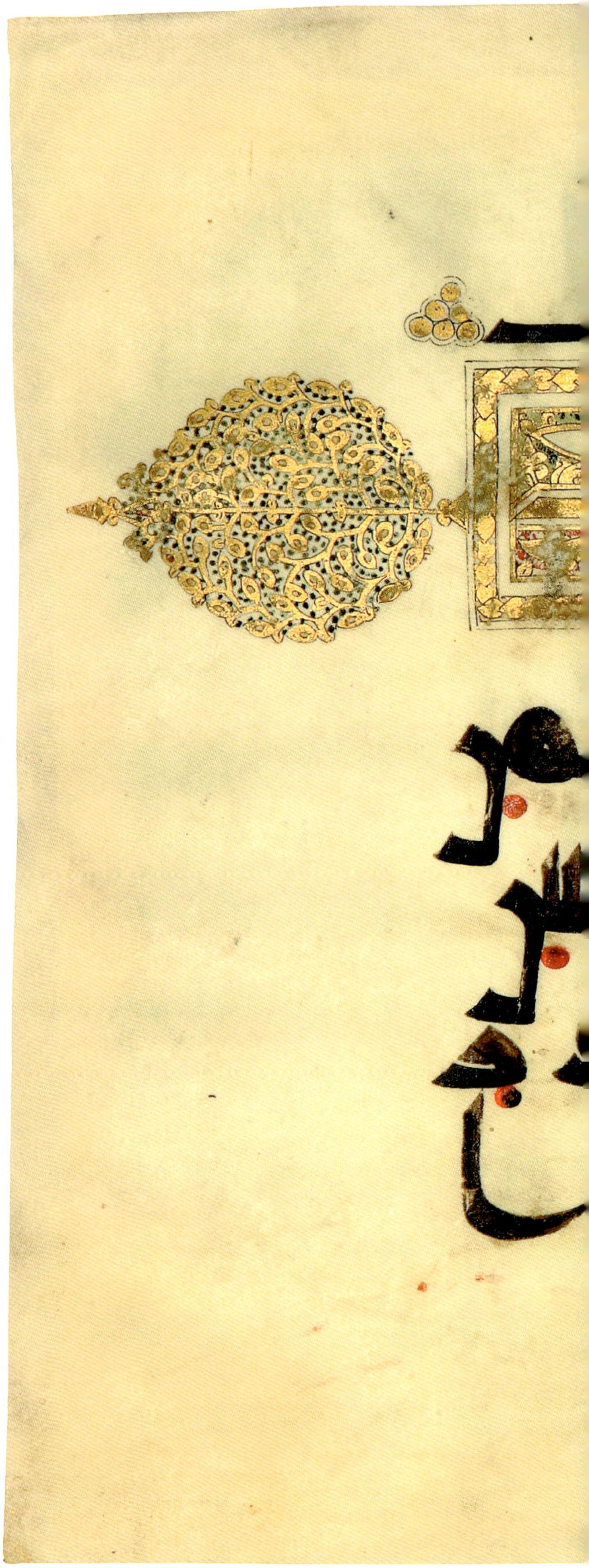

فاذ ٮک

[ornamental band]

ساا لا
ىال حلم
و ا لو ر د
 ىل ر ٯ

16
Leaf in Kufic script
North Africa or Near East
9th century CE
Surah 16 (*al-Nahl*) v. 69 – Surah 17 (*al-Isra'*) v. 34

Folio from an Arabic manuscript on parchment, eighteen lines of brown Kufic script per page; occasional letter-pointing in form of dashes; tenth verse markers in form of red roundels; *surah* headings in red Kufic script

13.6 × 18.4 cm

This Qur'an leaf, with eighteen lines of compact Kufic script within a small page, is remarkable for its entirely unadorned simplicity. With simple verse markers in the form of red roundels and very sparse letter-pointing in the form of dashes, it confirms the opinion that the owners of such manuscripts must already have been familiar with the Qur'anic text.

In François Déroche's classification of Qur'an scripts, this lies somewhere between groups B and D. It retains some of the archaisms of some of the Group B styles, such as a slight slope to the right of the vertical shafts of the letters and a generally small and compact appearance (Déroche 1992, pp. 35–36). Otherwise, the letter forms largely correspond to Group D, though they do not have the spaciousness and horizontal stretching (*mashq*) associated with that group.

17
Leaf in Kufic script
Near East, perhaps Iran
9th century CE
Surah 22 (*al-Hajj*), v. 5

Folio from an Arabic manuscript on parchment, seven lines of dark brown Kufic script per page; vocalization in form of green and red dots; outer margin has been trimmed

28 × 33 cm

This leaf is notable for its rather broad and free Kufic hand, clearly executed without any guidelines. According to François Déroche this leaf may have been part of the famous Ms. 322 in the Institute of Oriental Studies in St Petersburg. Another leaf from the same Qur'an is in the Nasser D. Khalili Collection (Déroche 1992, no. 69). For the St Petersburg manuscript, see al-Munajjid 1960, pl. 1.

ياتٮ ڡـلكم
ٮٯر علمٮـاه مں
مـكـں ڡلـوه
كـوڡلـه لـلڡـ
لا ٯحـ ماسـا
الو احــل مسو

18
Folio in Kufic script
Near East or North Africa
9th century CE
Surah 3 (*Al 'Imran*), vv. 136–40

Folio from an Arabic manuscript on parchment, seven lines of elongated brown Kufic script per page; possibly later letter-pointing in dark brown ink; vocalization in form of red dots; gold verse markers

25 × 33.1 cm

Like nos. 11 and 15, this leaf is in the mature 'Abbasid script classified by François Déroche as D.I. Typical features of this style visible here are the firm control of the proportions and the horizontal stretching (*mashq*). The script here has an angularity which is heightened by the use of the thin edge of the nib in the upper shaft of the letter *kaf* and the initial form of the letter *'ayn*. In this respect the leaf can be compared to a leaf formerly in the Schriftmuseum Rudolf Blanckertz, Berlin (Kühnel 1972, p. 6), and a leaf in the British Library (Safadi 1978, no. 15). The letter-pointing, not typical on manuscripts of this type, where preservation of the pristine surface of the page was often deemed more important, may well be a later addition.

Many of the most famous manuscripts in this script, such as the Qur'ans of Amajur and 'Abd al-Mun'im, have been donated to institutions (see Déroche 1992, p. 69). This leaf is almost certainly from the same manuscript as one in the Bodleian Library, illustrated by Yasin Dutton in his account of the use of diacritical marks in early Kufic Qur'ans (see Dutton 2000).

19
Folio in Kufic script
North Africa or Western Mediterranean
9th century CE
Surah 11 (*Hud*), vv. 47–58

Folio from an Arabic manuscript on parchment, thirteen lines of dark brown Kufic script per page; occasional use of letter-pointing in brown ink; vocalization in form of red dots; tenth verse divisions marked with illuminated square devices containing a letter with the appropriate *abjad* value; defective with losses at lower edges, mounted in paper borders

14.1 × 26 cm

This folio can be confidently attributed to North Africa or the Western Mediterranean region owing to the use of the letter *sad* for verse 60 of Surah 11 (*Hud*). The letter *sad* is used for the value 60 only in the western *abjad* system, whereas the eastern system uses the letter *sin* (Stanley 1995, p. 18). The script is closest to group D.IV in François Déroche's classification of 'Abbasid scripts (Déroche 1992, pp. 37, 44–45). This script is associated with mature 'Abbasid manuscripts with a large number of lines to the page.

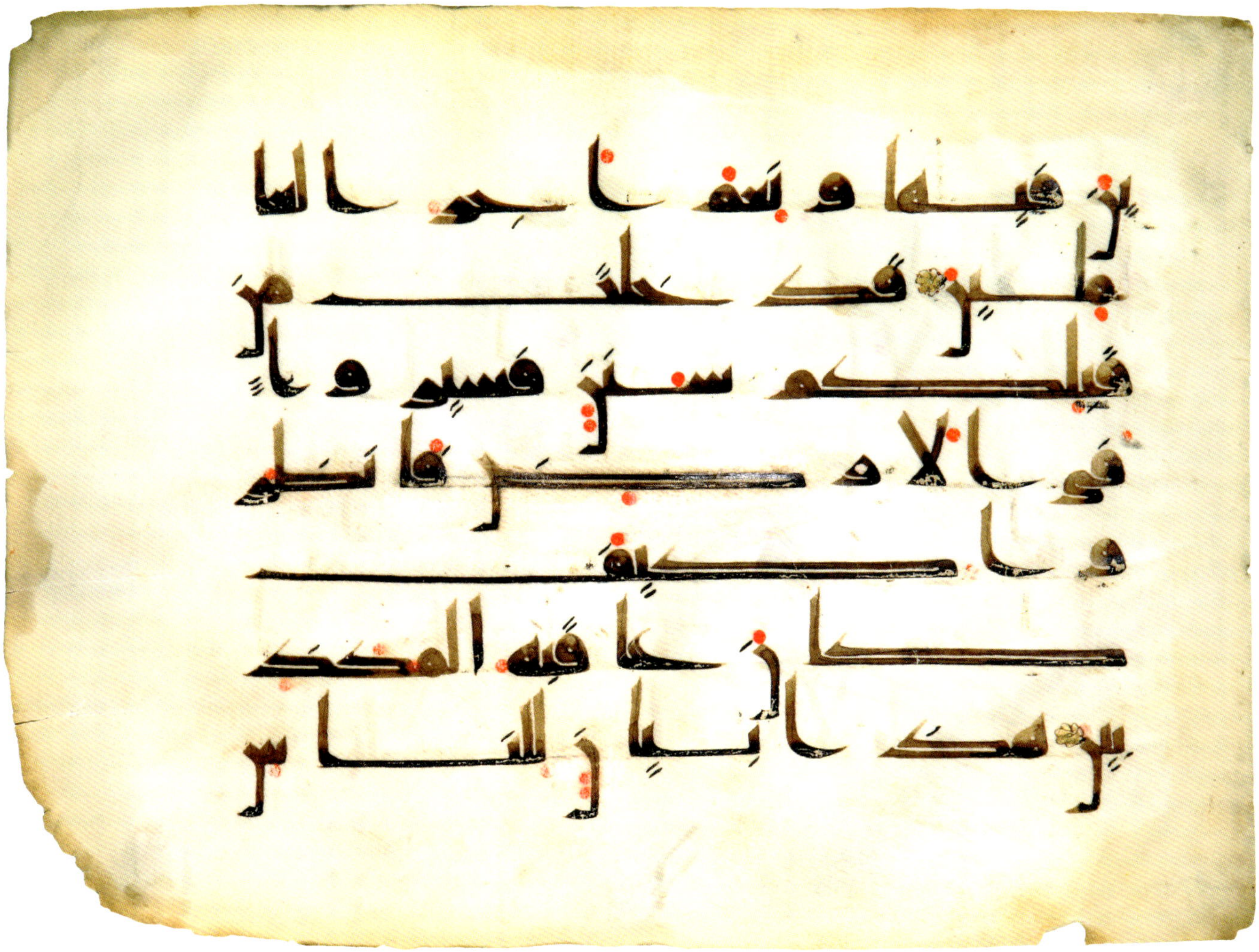

18

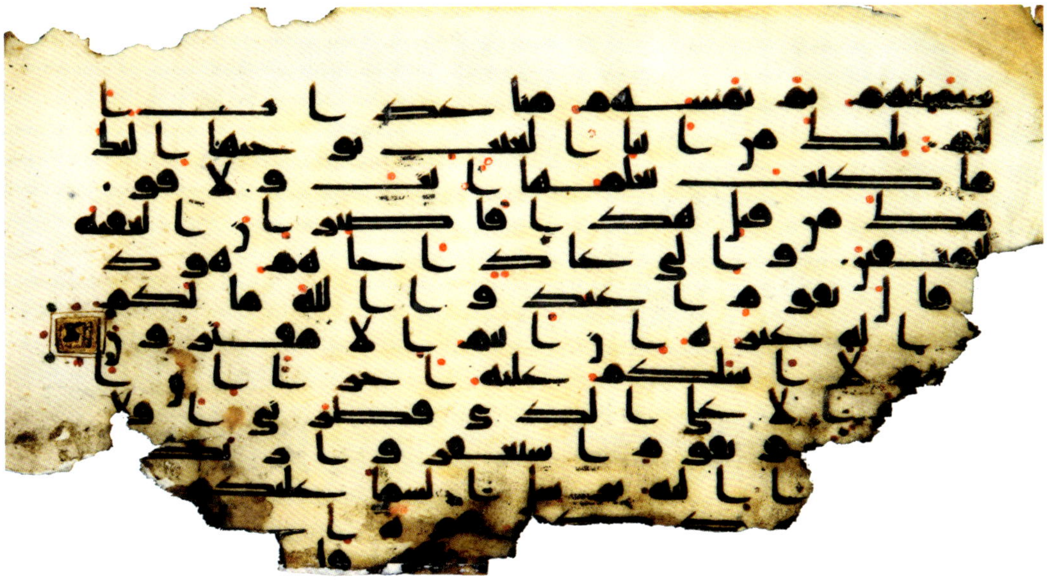

19

20
Leaf in Kufic script
Near East or North Africa
9th – 10th century CE
Surah 7 *(al A'raf)*, vv. 128–36

Folio from an Arabic manuscript on vellum, thirteen lines of dark brown Kufic script per page; vocalization in form of red dots; verse markers in form of fine diagonal strokes; verse 130 marked with an illuminated device in colours and gold, in the middle of which the verse count is given in *abjad*

20.5 × 33 cm

This leaf belongs to group D.IV in François Déroche's classification of 'Abbasid scripts (Déroche 1992, pp. 37, 44–45). Although the text block is quite dense, there is an elegant use of *mashq* that gives a feeling of spaciousness.

A bifolium from the same manuscript appeared at Bonhams, 17 October 2002, lot 8.

21
Leaf in gold Kufic script
Near East or North Africa
9th century CE
Surah 19 (*Maryam*), vv. 59–61

Folio from an Arabic manuscript on parchment, five lines of Kufic script in gold outlined in brown per page; vocalization in form of red dots, green and blue dots; individual verses marked with gold rosettes circled in blue

14.5 × 20 cm

This leaf comes from a famous manuscript written entirely in gold, known to have once been housed in Qayrawan. According to Ibn al-Nadim, writing in the tenth century, the practice of copying the Qur'an was introduced by the Caliph 'Umar, who was inspired by the gold inscription on the mosque in Medina (see no. 10). The use of gold ink, a luxury that could only be afforded by the very affluent, may indicate that the manuscript was commissioned by a wealthy member of society, or even a caliph.

Other leaves from the same manuscript are found in various public and private collections, including the Bibliothèque nationale, Paris; the Bibliothèque nationale and the Institut national d'archeologie et arts, Tunis; Beit al-Qur'an, Bahrain; the Tareq Rajab Museum and the al-Sabah Collection, Kuwait; the Nasser D. Khalili Collection, and the Victoria and Albert Museum, London (for a partial list, see Déroche 1992, p. 67).

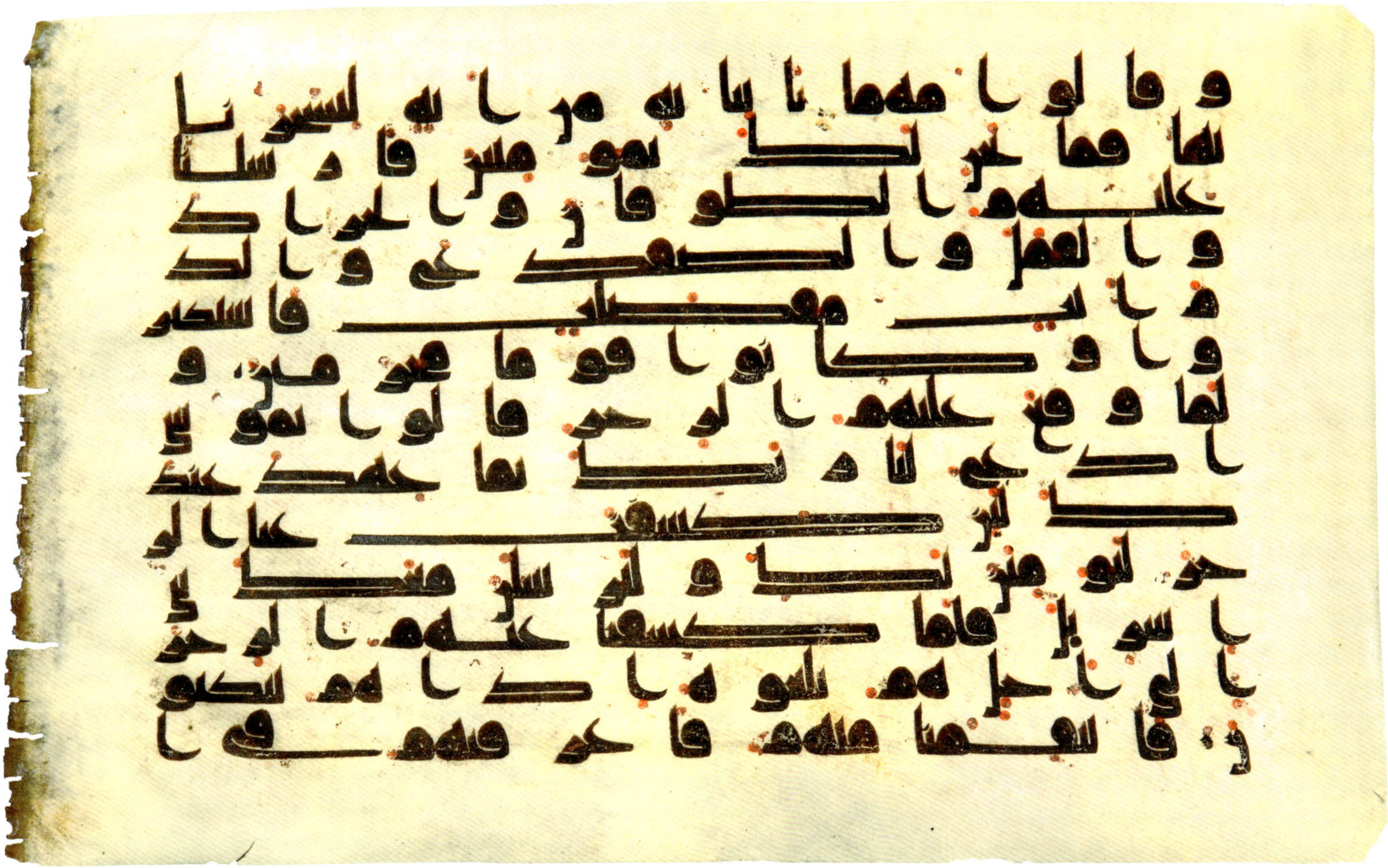

20

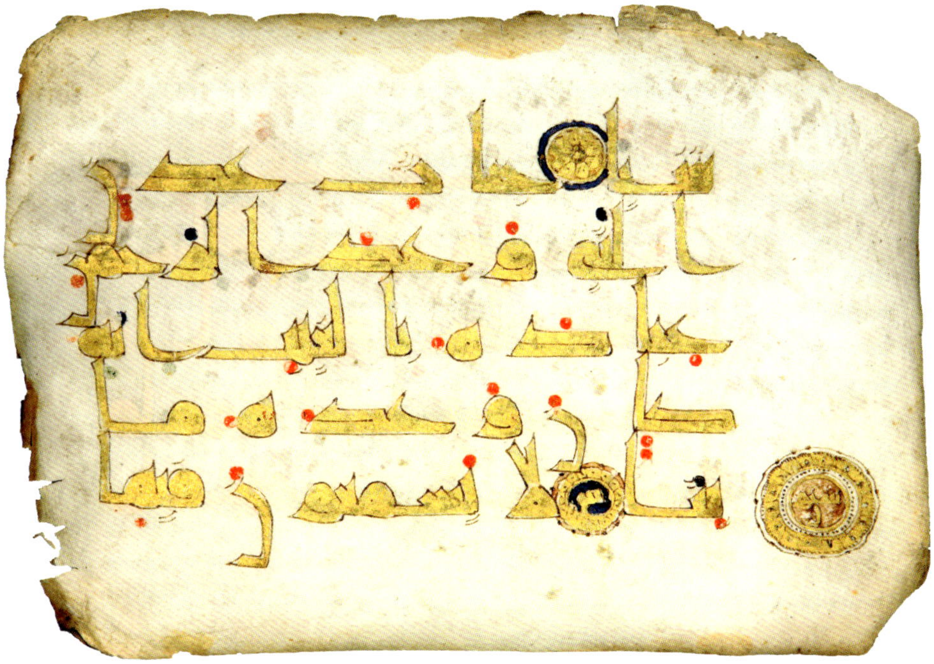

21

نا ها ا لا
ولغا لو الا
ما فو ا د ا
ك و ا
ا ع لا
و ع ا ل د ا ز
م هل و ا لـ

22
Folio in Kufic script
Near East or North Africa
Late 9th century CE
Surah 33 (*al-Ahzab*), vv. 59–61

Leaf from an Arabic manuscript on parchment, seven lines of dark brown Kufic script per page; vocalization in form of red, yellow and green dots; single verse divisions are marked with triangular arrangements of gold dots; tenth verse divisions are marked with roundels in red and gold containing the exact verse count in gold Kufic script

27.2 × 36.2 cm

This leaf belongs to a group of manuscripts written in an aesthetically highly developed Kufic script, characterized by highly controlled proportions and strong horizontal stretching (*mashq*) of letters and ligatures (see also nos. 11, 15, 18).

The script of this large leaf is very close to that of the well-known Amajur Qur'an, a manuscript on parchment given as a *waqf* to a mosque in Tyre by the 'Abbasid governor of Damascus, Amajur, in 875–76 CE (illustrated in Ettinghausen *et al.* 2001, fig. 118). A dating for the present bifolium in the second half of the ninth century is further supported by several other Qur'ans written in a similar script which are either dated or have dated *waqf* inscriptions ranging from 847 to 911 (see Déroche 1992, pp. 36–37).

Two other folios from this manuscript are in the Musée des arts islamiques, Qayrawan.

23
Bifolium in Kufic script
North Africa or Western Mediterranean
Late 9th century CE
Surah 10 (*Yunus*), vv. 101–09 – Surah 11 (*Hud*), vv. 1–4

Bifolium from an Arabic manuscript on parchment, ten lines of brown Kufic script per page; vocalization in form of red dots; *hamzat al-wasl* and *hamzat al-qat'* in form of blue and yellow dots; *shaddah* in form of red semi-circle; long *alif* in form of red line; further markings in blue and red; single verse divisions are marked with a small triangular cluster of three red, yellow and blue dots; fifth verse divisions marked with a stylized letter ha in gold; *surah* heading in gold and silver Kufic script outlined in dark brown ink with a gold stylized palmette extending into the margin; the word hizb is written vertically next to the palmette in black ink

17.5 × 26 cm

The script of this bifolium is closest to styles D.II and D.III of Déroche's system of categorization. This script is associated with the second half of the ninth century and the early tenth century (Déroche 1992, pp. 14, 26, 28, 29, 35). It is interesting to note that the leaf does not share the same aesthetic considerations as other manuscripts in this group, but rather appears neat and essentially functional.

The manuscript makes use of a vocalization system that has been associated with the Western Mediterranean and the Maghrib. This consists of a *shaddah* symbol in the form of a hemicircle, and a red dash to mark a long unwritten *alif* (Blair 2006, p. 122; see also nos. 14, 26, 28, 29, 35). These have been supplemented here with a red or blue horizontal dash to mark *wasl* and a blue hemicircle to occasionally to mark a *fatha*.

The *surah* heading on the manuscript is unusual in that the *surah* title and the numbers of verses are written in alternating gold and silver script. Text in alternating colours is also a feature of nos. 29 and 35, both of which also make use of the the system of hemicircles and vertical dashes. This may suggest that text in alternating colours of ink is also an indication of a western Islamic origin.

On the third line of folio 1r the scribe has corrected a mistake in the text by erasing the original letters by scraping the parchment and rewriting them.

24
Leaf in Kufic script
Near East or North Africa
Late 9th century CE
Surah 46 (*al-Ahqaf*), vv. 21–22

Folio from an Arabic manuscript on parchment, five lines of dark brown Kufic script per page; vocalization in form of red dots; tenth verse marker in form of an ornate illuminated roundel

22 × 31 cm

This script on this leaf is closest to the style classified as D.III by François Déroche (see Déroche 1992, pp. 36–37). Like D.I, this style is associated with luxurious Qur'ans with few lines of text to the page. The scripts are similar, though D.III is characterized by a distinctly flattened lower return on the independent form of the letter *alif* (Déroche 1992, p. 43).

Manuscripts in this style are dated between the late ninth and early tenth century. Unusually for Qur'ans belonging to the D group, the letter-pointing on this leaf appears to be original. The script and dimensions compare closely to a leaf in the Musée des Arts Islamiques, Qayrawan, which also has original letter-pointing (Paris 1982, no. 331; Lings and Safadi 1976, no. 10). A leaf from the same manuscript was exhibited in the Museum für Islamische Kunst, Berlin, in 2006 (Fraser and Kwiatkowski 2006, no. 9).

23

24

25
Folio in Kufic script
Near East or North Africa
10th century CE
Surah 33 (*al-Ahzab*), vv. 19–20

Folio from an Arabic manuscript on parchment, five lines of dark brown Kufic script per page; letter-pointing in form of dark strokes; vocalization in form of red, green, yellow and blue dots; individual verse division marked with illuminated rosette

23 × 31.5 cm

Like no. 24, this leaf is in style D.III according to Déroche's classification of 'Abbasid scripts. Manuscripts in this style are generally luxurious copies with few lines of text to the page.

A folio from the same manuscript is in the Bibliothèque nationale, Paris (Paris 2001, no. 58). A further leaf is at the Museum für Islamische Kunst, Berlin (Mainz am Rhein 2001, p. 131).

لا إله إلا
الله يخشون
الرحمن
بالغيب

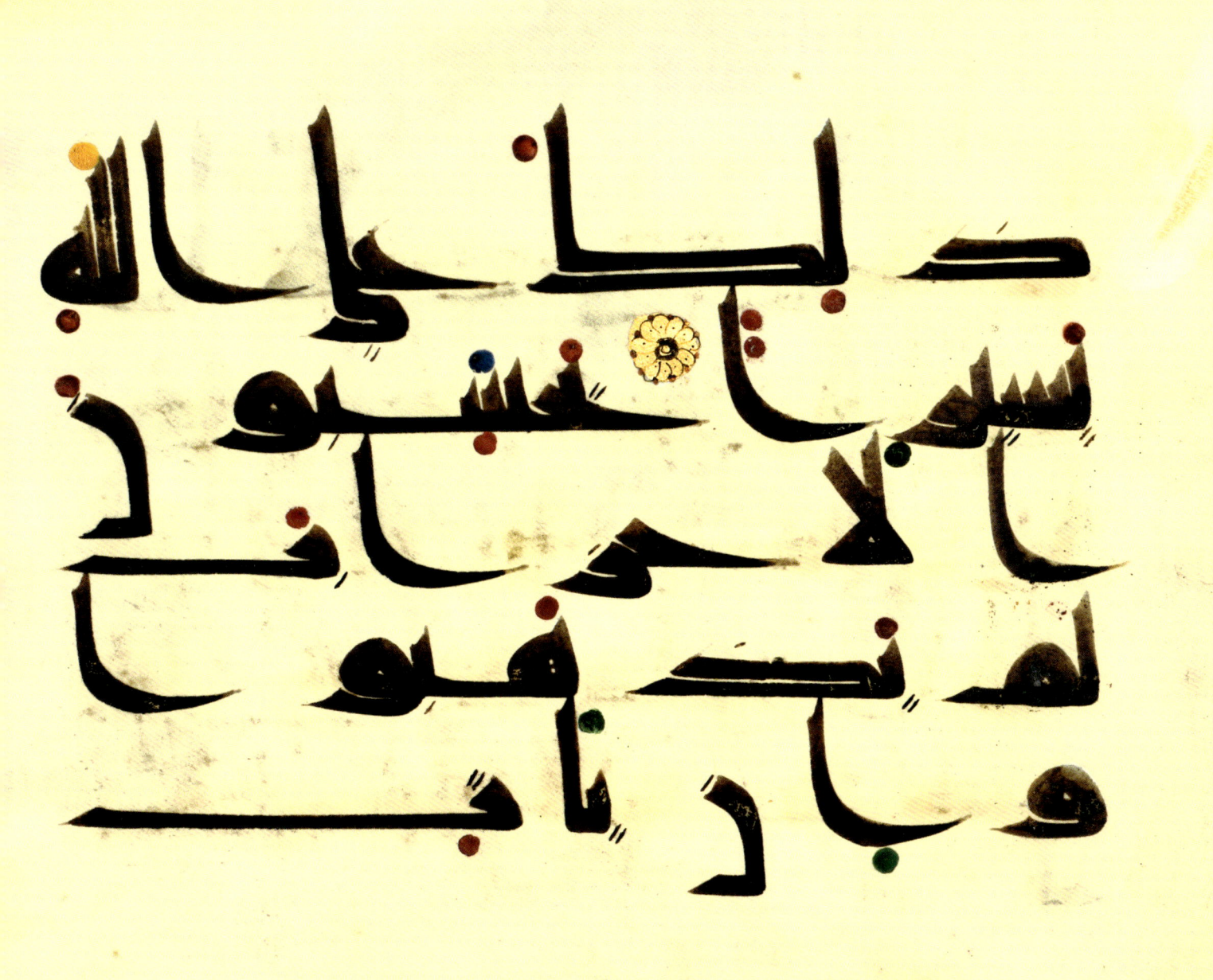

26
Monumental leaf in Kufic script
North Africa or Western Mediterranean
9th – 10th century CE
Surah 14 (*Ibrahim*) vv. 40–end – Surah 15 (*al-Hijr*) vv. 1–31

Folio from an Arabic manuscript on parchment, eighteen lines of Kufic script in brown ink per page; vocalization in form of red dots; *shaddah* symbol in form of a red semi-circle, long medial *alif* marked with a red vertical stroke; *surah* heading marked with verse count in red, with the final ligature of the word *ayah* (verse) stretching to the end of the line; tenth verse divisions are marked with a simple red circle

39.7 × 54 cm

The script on this large leaf falls largely into group D according to François Déroche's classification of 'Abbasid scripts. Certain features, however, such as the deeply curved terminal *nun*, and an occasional *alif* with a short upward-turning return, are closer to those of style C.I. There are certain other idiosyncrasies, most notably the spike-like extensions to the ends of the final forms of the letters *waw*, *nun* and *ra*. This feature is found on other manuscripts with scripts showing a mixture of characteristics from groups C and D (see nos. 12, 29, 35).

It has been argued that the text was initially devoid of vocalization or diacritics, and that these were added at a slightly later date. On the basis of its sparse appearance and spatial economy, it has been suggested that the manuscript was made for an institution of learning (Fraser and Kwiatkowski 2006, p. 36). The use of a hemicircle as a *shaddah* symbol and a stroke for long unwritten *alifs* are orthographic practices that have been attributed to North Africa and the Western Mediterranean (Blair 2006, p. 122, and nos. 14, 23, 29, 35).

A folio from the manuscript was published by Bernard Quaritch Ltd in 1995 (Stanley 1995, no. 2). Further leaves have appeared at Sotheby's, 6 April 2011, lot 166; 1 April 2009, lot 3; 8 October 2008, lot 7; 9 April 2008, lot 14; 24 October 2007, lot 3. Two leaves from the same manuscript were exhibited in the Museum für Islamische Kunst, Berlin, 2006 (Fraser and Kwiatkowski 2006, no. 6).

دوي ۞ ولا تهنوا في ابتغاء القوم ان تكونوا تالمون فانهم يالمون كما تالمون وترجون من الله ما لا يرجون وكان الله عليما حكيما ۞ انا انزلنا اليك الكتاب بالحق لتحكم بين الناس بما اراك الله ولا تكن للخائنين خصيما ۞ واستغفر الله ان الله كان غفورا رحيما ۞ ولا تجادل عن الذين يختانون انفسهم ان الله لا يحب من كان خوانا اثيما ۞ يستخفون من الناس ولا يستخفون من الله وهو معهم اذ يبيتون ما لا يرضى من القول وكان الله بما يعملون محيطا ۞ ها انتم هولاء جادلتم عنهم في الحيوة الدنيا فمن يجادل الله عنهم يوم القيمة ام من يكون عليهم وكيلا ۞ ومن يعمل سوءا او يظلم نفسه ثم يستغفر الله يجد الله غفورا رحيما ۞ ومن يكسب اثما فانما يكسبه على نفسه وكان الله عليما حكيما ۞ ومن يكسب خطيئة او اثما ثم يرم به بريئا فقد احتمل بهتانا واثما مبينا ۞

الحمد لله رب العالمين

بسم الله الرحمن الرحيم المائدة

27
Leaf in gold Kufic script on blue parchment
North Africa or Western Mediterranean
9th – 10th century CE
Surah 2 (*al-Baqarah*), vv. 261–67

Folio from an Arabic manuscript on blue-dyed parchment, fifteen lines of gold Kufic script per page; no vocalization; only three instances of original letter-pointing with short diagonal gold dashes; single verse divisions are marked with small silver florets (now oxidized to black); traces of a fifth verse marker in the lower right corner of the verso in form of an illuminated roundel; faint trace of a large illuminated roundel marking a *hizb* division in the upper left margin of the recto

25 × 37 cm

This leaf comes from one of the most famous and luxurious Kufic Qur'an manuscripts, the unique blue and gold design of which has engendered much scholarly speculation. The most recent studies agree in assigning an origin in the Islamic West. Certain features, such as the scoring of a grid of lines into the vellum to guide the calligrapher and the use of the letter *sad* for the number 60 in the *abjad* system, appear to be found only in manuscripts from Islamic North Africa and Spain (see no. 19).

More specifically, using Fatimid sources and the library inventory from the Great Mosque in Qayrawan, where the manuscript was stored from as early as 1294 CE, Jonathan Bloom has suggested Fatimid-ruled Ifriqiyyah. Roughly corresponding to modern-day Tunisia, this was the centre of Fatimid power in 909–69, and Bloom suggests the manuscript was produced there for one of the cultured rulers of the mid tenth century, such as al-Mansur (r. 946–53) or al-Mu'izz (r. 953–75) (Bloom 1989).

Tim Stanley has added Islamic Spain as another possible origin, pointing to inscriptions in gold Kufic on red and blue-black grounds in the Great Mosque of Cordoba (Stanley 1995, pp. 14–15). More recently, Marcus Fraser has proposed Sicily. Fraser suggests that the unique use of a blue-black parchment may have been in response to and in competition with Christian manuscripts on purple-dyed vellum. Fraser cites the example of the Rossano Gospels, which were made by a Byzantine scriptorium some time in the sixth century and made their way to Calabria in South Italy probably in the eighth century. He suggests that such manuscripts may have been seen by Muslim dynasties such as the Kalbids or the Aghlabids, who ruled Sicily and periodically parts of Calabria and Puglia in the ninth and tenth centuries (Fraser and Kwiatkowski 2006, pp. 44–48). Whatever the precise origins of the manuscript, it is clear that the manuscript was commissioned by a ruler of great wealth and artistic daring and sophistication.

The bulk of the manuscript is in Tunisia, divided between the Bibliothèque nationale and the Musée des Arts Islamiques. Individual pages began to appear on the art market in the early part of the twentieth century, and are found in numerous museums, including the Fogg Art Museum, Harvard University; the Museum of Fine Arts, Boston; the Chester Beatty Library, Dublin; the David Collection, Copenhagen; the Aga Khan Museum; and numerous private collections.

For a selection of other published pages, see Geneva 1985, no. 3; Doha 2008, no. 5; Wright 2009, fig. 67.

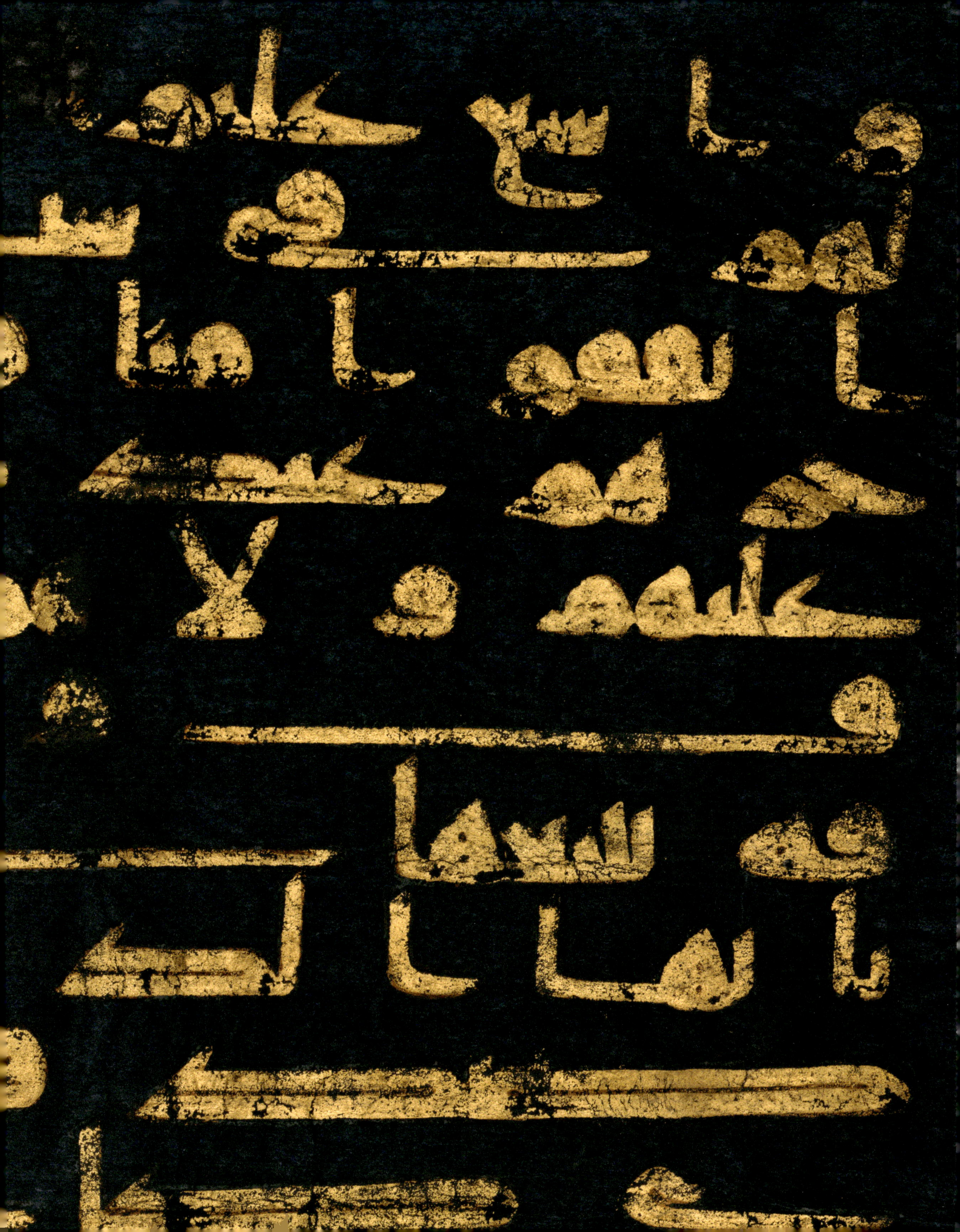

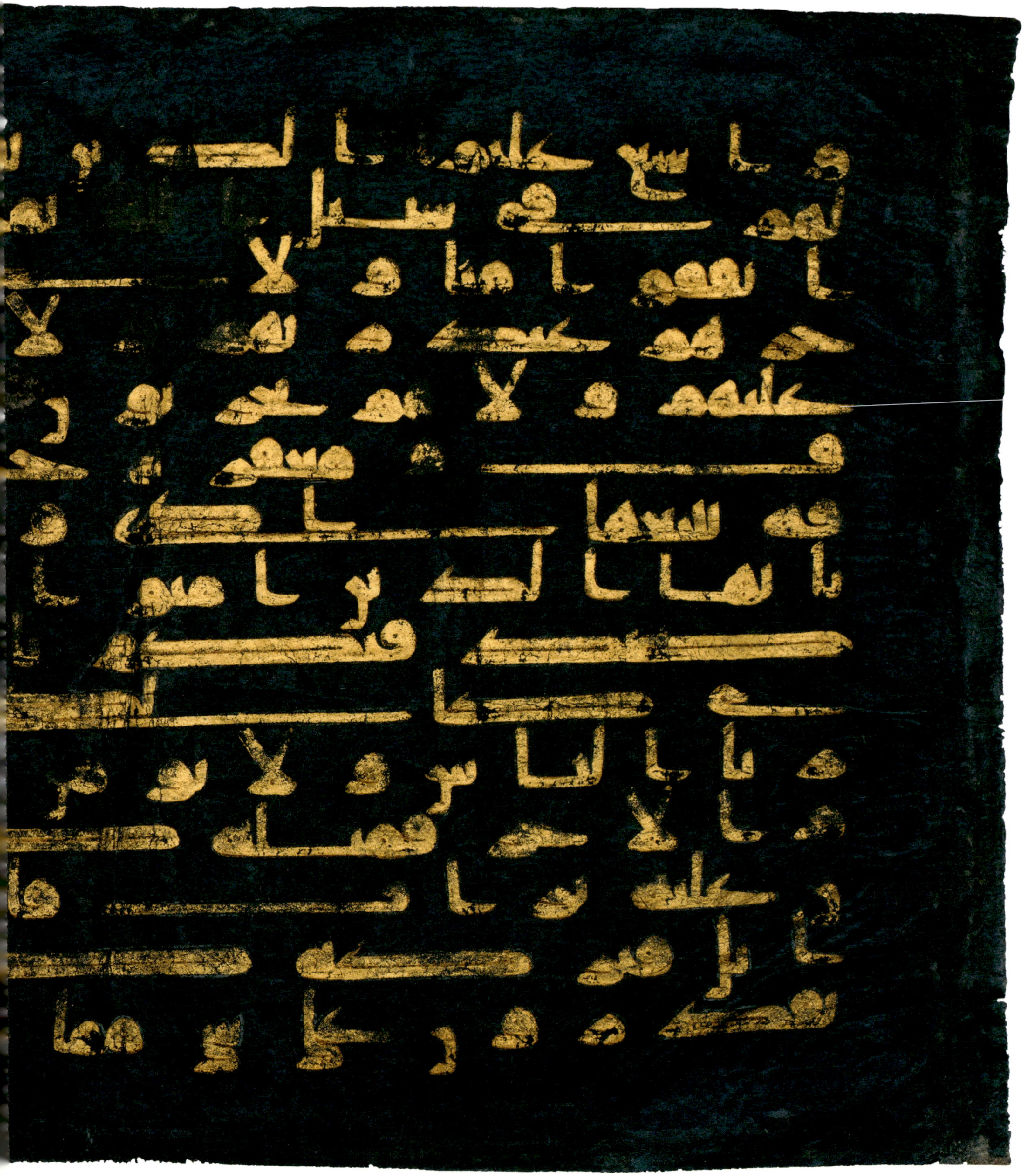

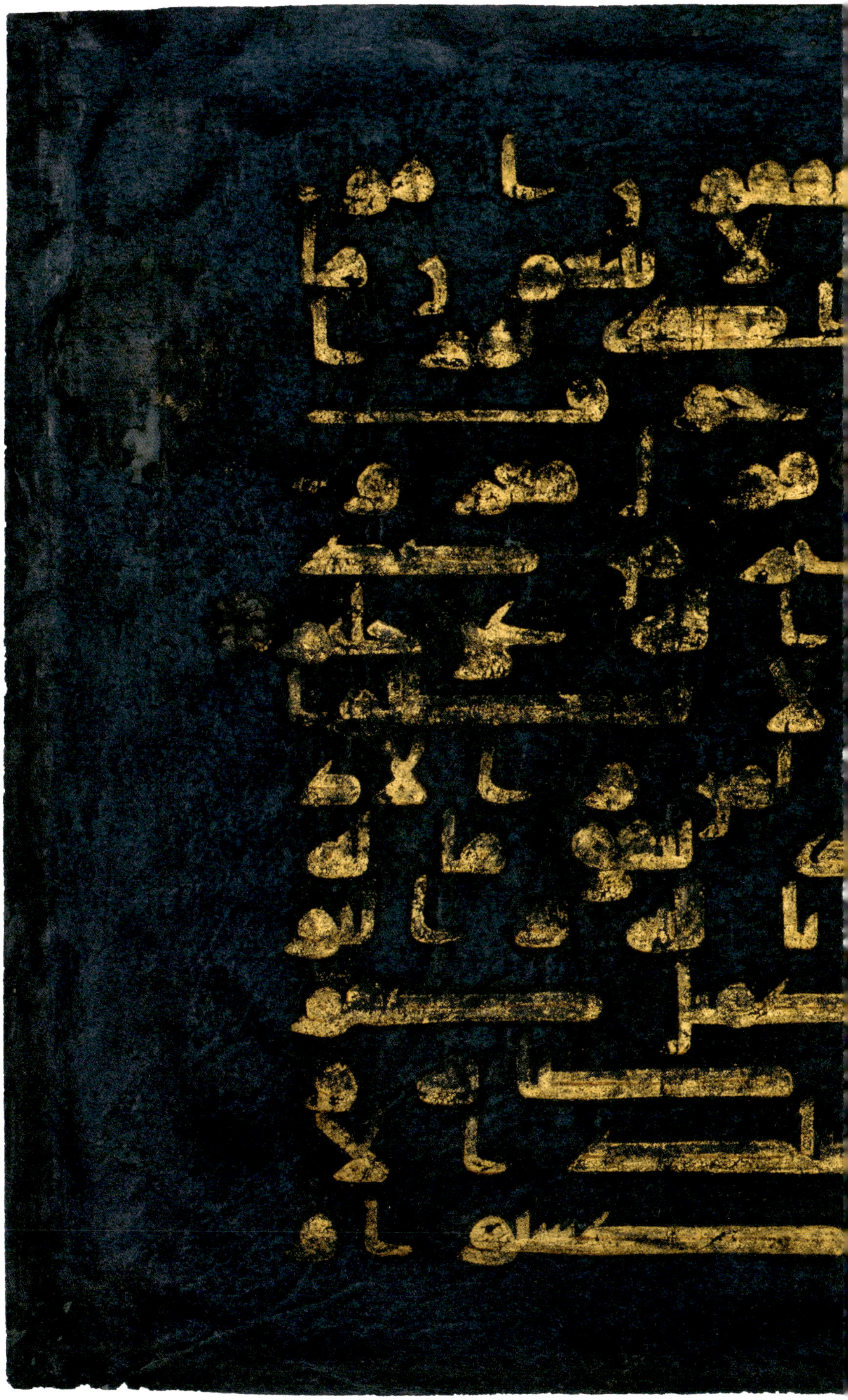

28
Leaf in Kufic script
Near East or North Africa
10th century CE
Surah 22 (*al-Hajj*), v. 7 – Surah 23 (*al-Mu'minun*), vs. 17

Folio from an Arabic manuscript on parchment, sixteen lines of brown Kufic script per page; vocalization in form of red dots; later diacritics and long medial *alifs* in green; *surah* heading consisting of title and verse count in gold Kufic with a gold and polychrome palmette extending into the margin; end of the seventeenth *juz'* marked in gold Kufic above *surah* heading; fifth verse division marked with gold *ha*-shaped device; tenth verse division marked with gold rosette with blue centre

18 × 25.4 cm

The palmette issuing from the *surah* heading on this leaf is decorated with a colourful and unusual green and gold checked pattern. While checked patterns are not uncommon on frontispieces and *surah* dividers in Kufic Qur'ans, their use is rarely extended to the marginal palmettes. For another example, see a palmette in a Kufic Qur'an in the Museum of Turkish and Islamic Arts (Istanbul 2010a, no. 38), with a small red and white checked centre. Another unusual feature is the marking of the end of the seventeenth *juz'* in gold letters in the line above the *surah* heading.

The script on the leaf is related to group D.IV in François Déroche's classification of 'Abbasid scripts.

29
Bifolium in Kufic script
North Africa or Western Mediterranean
9th – 10th century CE
Surah 49 (*al-Hujarat*), v. 14 – Surah 50 (*Qaf*), v. 12

Bifolium from an Arabic manuscript on vellum, nine lines of Kufic script in brown ink per page; vocalization in form of red dots; *hamzat al-wasl* and *hamzat al-qat'* marked with blue and yellow dots; long *alif* marked with red line; *shaddah* in form of red semi-circle; *surah* heading with title (*Qaf*) and verse count in alternating green, yellow and red Kufic script; individual verse divisions marked with small vertical rows of four diagonal dashes; fifth verse divisions marked with gold and polychrome *ha*-shaped devices; tenth verses marked by quatrefoil motifs in blue, red and yellow

19.6 × 27 cm

The *surah* heading on this Qur'an leaf has been written in an unusual combination of alternating green, yellow and red inks. Text in alternating colours is also a feature of nos. 23 and 35, both of which also employ orthographic features that have been linked to the Maghrib and Western Mediterranean. These consist of a *shaddah* symbol in the form of a hemicircle and a long, unwritten *alif* in the form of a vertical stroke (Blair 2006, p. 122; and nos. 14, 23, 26, 29, 35). The coincidence of these features in all three cases along with text in alternating colours may suggest that the latter too is a feature of western Islamic manuscripts. The word *hubs*, the western Islamic word for a pious endowment, has been inscribed with pinpricks in the space above the text.

The script on the leaf falls into group D in François Déroche's classification of 'Abbasid scripts. The ornamental script of the *surah* heading exhibits characteristics of other scripts, however, most strikingly in the case of the letter *qaf*, the sublinear part of which drops to the line below, as in scripts in group C.

A leaf from this manuscript was sold at Sotheby's, 6 April 2011, lot 179.

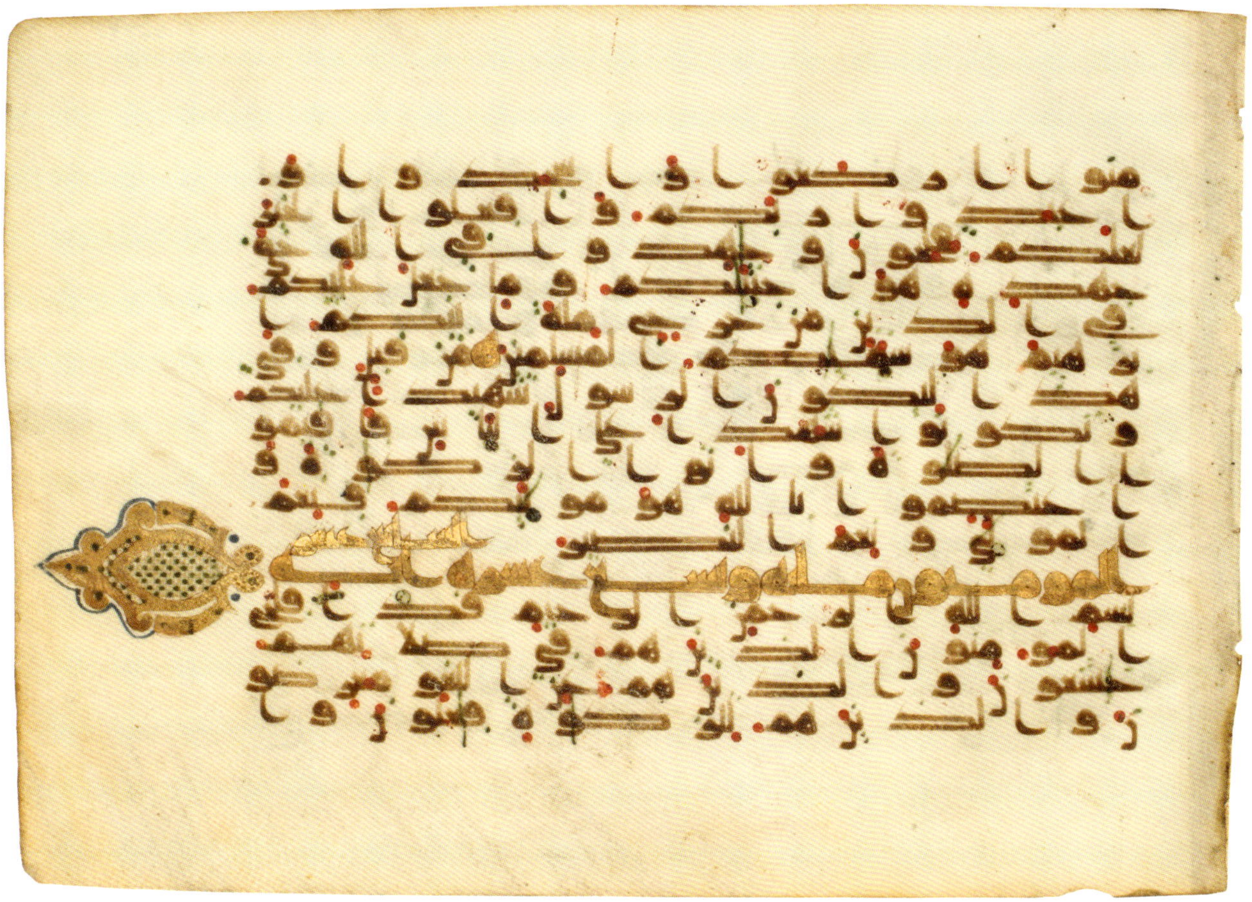

28

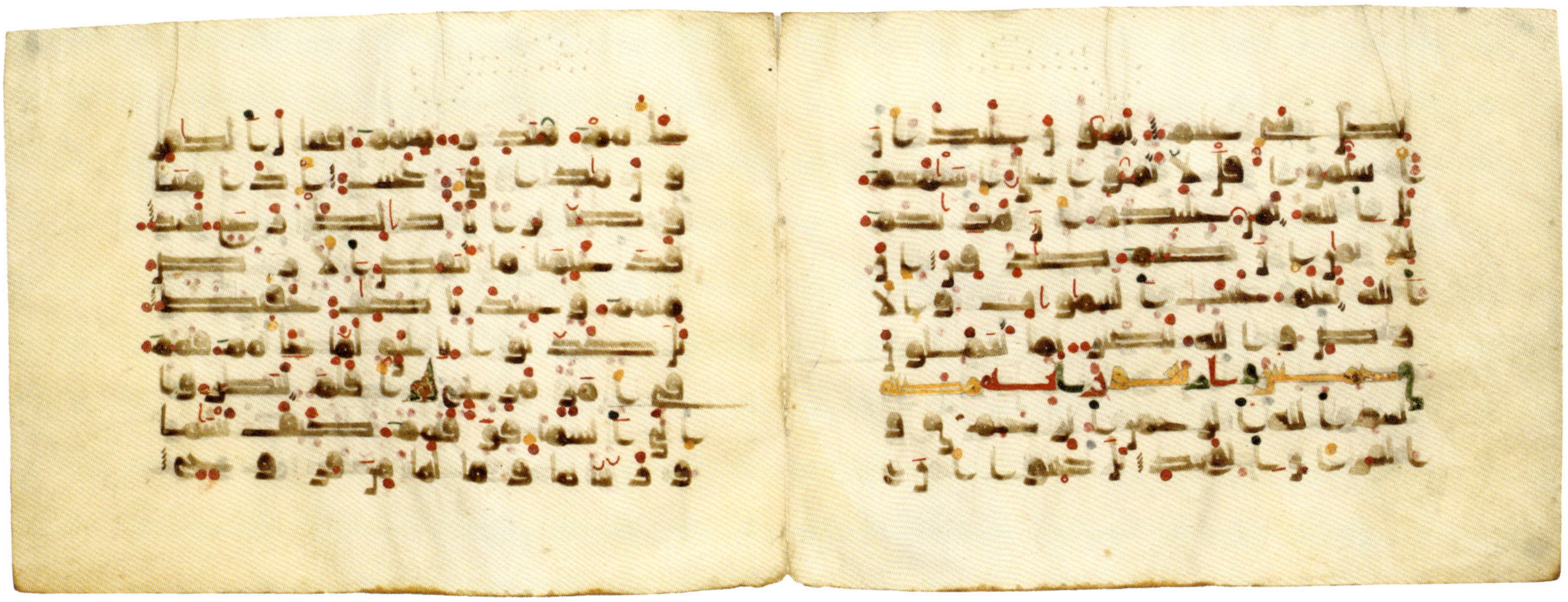

29

30
Leaf in gold Kufic script
Near East or North Africa
9th – 10th century CE
Surah 13 (*al-Ra'd*), vv. 38–40

Folio from an Arabic manuscript on parchment, seven lines of Kufic script in gold outlined in dark brown per page; vocalization in form of red and green dots; verse markers in form of small gold rosettes

14.5 × 20 cm

The practice of chrysography, or writing in gold, was supposedly introduced by the Caliph 'Umar, who was said to have been inspired by the mosque in Medina (see no. 10). It was both very costly and time consuming, requiring the scribe to write the letters out with glue before applying the gold and outlining the letters in sepia. There are famous examples of early Qur'ans with five, nine and fifteen lines of gold script to the page (see e.g. nos. 10, 21, 27). This page, however, comes from a little-known manuscript with seven.

وإذا سلّام وقالوا سلاماً وحسبهم وهو ولم يكن لهم ولد ولوط إذ قال لقومه

31
Bifolium in Kufic script
Near East or North Africa
9th or early 10th century CE
Surah 24 (*al-Nur*), vv. 53–55

Bifolium from an Arabic manuscript on parchment, six lines of dark brown Kufic script per page; vocalization in form of red dots; tenth verse division marked with a small gold roundel within a double ring of brown ink

11 × 16.8 cm

The script on this fine white parchment bifolium is closest to the D.Va group according to François Déroche's classification of Kufic scripts (Déroche 1992, pp. 43–45). A characteristic of this script is a slight vertical stretching of the letter forms, most visible here in the first line of each page.

Leaves from this group are largely dated between the late ninth and early tenth century. For a Qur'an leaf in a comparable script, see Déroche 1992, no. 45.

32
Leaf in Kufic script
Near East or North Africa
9th or early 10th century CE
Surah 28 (*al-Qasas*), vv. 74–76

Folio from an Arabic manuscript on parchment, nine lines of dark brown Kufic script per page; vocalization in form of red and occasional green dots; fifth verse divisions marked with stylized letter *ha* in gold; ink on verso worn

10.6 × 17 cm

The script on this Kufic leaf falls into the group D.Va in François Deroche's classification of Kufic scripts. As with no. 31, there is a slight vertical stretching of the letter forms in the first line of the page.

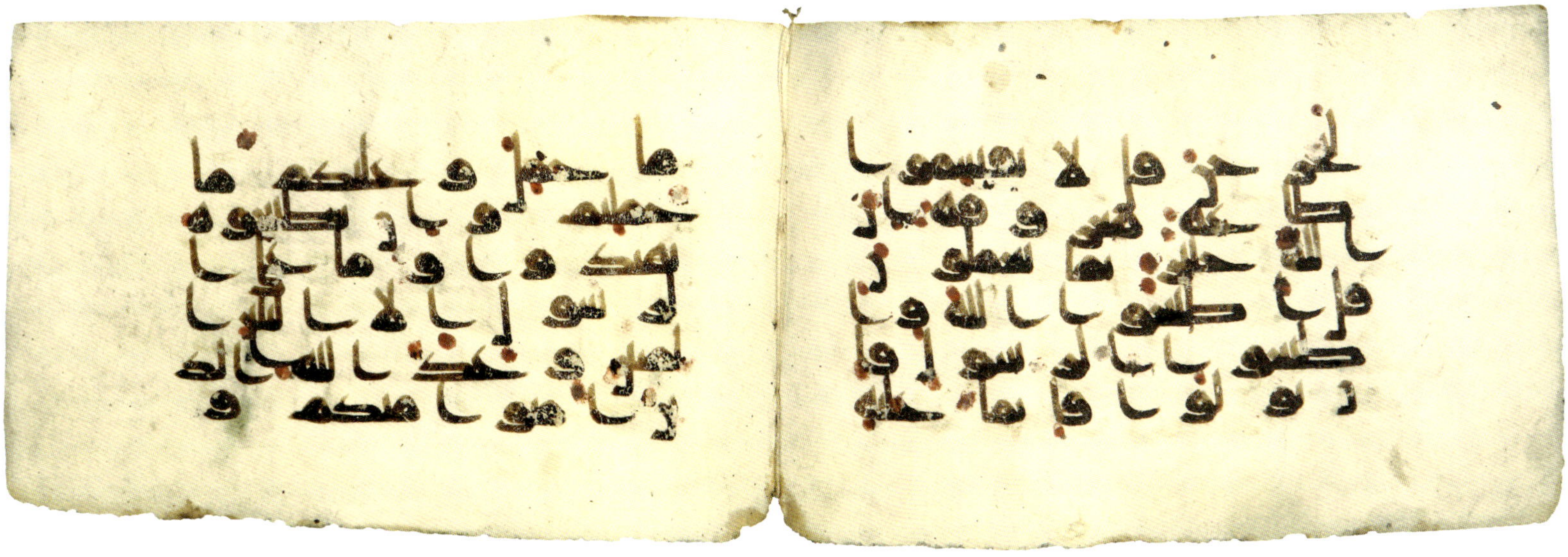
31

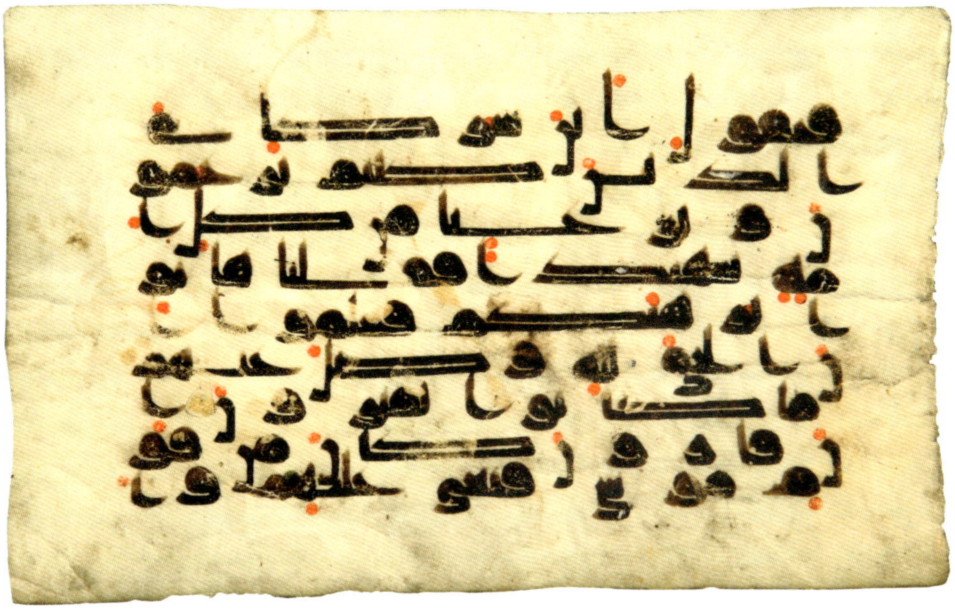
32

33
Leaf in Kufic script
Near East or North Africa
9th – 10th century CE
Surah 23 (*al-Mu'minun*), vv. 68–72

Folio from an Arabic manuscript on parchment, nine lines of dark brown Kufic script per page; vocalization in form of red dots; tenth verse division marked with illuminated roundel

11 × 18 cm

Like nos. 31 and 32, this small Qur'an leaf is in the style classified by François Déroche as D.Va. As with those leaves, there is a vertical stretching of the letter forms on the first line of the page.

34
Leaf in Kufic script
Near East or North Africa
9th – 10th century CE
Surah 80 (*'Abasa*), vv. 23–34

Folio from an Arabic manuscript on parchment, eight lines of dark brown Kufic script per page; vocalization in form of red and green dots; letter-pointing in form of brown dashes; fifth and tenth verse divisions marked with illuminated roundels

19 × 12.5 cm

The letter forms on this leaf are closest to those in group D.Va in François Déroche's classification of 'Abbasid scripts, though they do not have the horizontal stretching often associated with that script (see nos. 31–33). Manuscripts in this script are typically small with between seven and nine lines to the page (Déroche 1992, nos. 43–48, 50, 51).

33

ودنا طمه بكه وايا
لوكاها حاهما لمها
هم الاهه لاولبا
ماه قوه سوبا
لهم ولودروحه
لهو وذلي كلوهم
كالوه قاهم نهم وبا
اهوشاهم ولسك

34

لما نصر ما فوه قلسو
الاسادبالى حسامه اصلنا
اها صنا سهها الادص
سا فاشاهما خنا وحنا
قنا ودسو اولنلا وحدا
يو حلنا وفاكهه وانا
لكهم ولاسامصه فادا حا
باالصاحهنوه لوالمو

35
Leaf in Kufic script
Probably North Africa or Western Mediterranean
10th century CE
Surah 16 (*al-Nahl*), vv. 46–61

Folio from an Arabic manuscript on parchment, eleven lines of brown Kufic script per page; vocalization in form of red dots; *hamzat al-qat'* and *hamzat al-wasl* marked with yellow and blue dots; *shaddah* markers in form of red semi-circles; long medial *alifs* marked with red dashes; *sukun* markers in form of blue circles; individual verses divisions marked with vertical row of three blue dots; fifth verse division in form of stylized letter *ha* in red and gold; tenth verse division marked with gold and polychrome quatrefoil outlined in brown; *sajdah* marking in margin in form of a roundel with white Kufic script reserved against a red, brown and blue gound within a polychrome frame of repeated vegetal pattern; tenth verse and *hizb* division marked in polychrome Kufic letters below

16.8 × 26.6 cm

36
Leaf in Kufic script
Near East or North Africa
10th century CE
Surah 3 (*Al 'Imran*), vv. 190–94

Folio from an Arabic manuscript on parchment, eleven lines of dark brown Kufic script per page; vocalization in red; dark blue *shaddah* symbol in its modern form; green *hamzat al-qat'* in its modern form; individual verses marked with roundels containing word *ayah* (verse) in Kufic script reserved against a gold ground; tenth verse division marked with large gold roundel containing verse count (190) in Kufic script reserved against a gold ground

23.5 × 17 cm

Like that on no. 26, the script on this leaf belongs basically to group D according to François Déroche's classification of Abbasid scripts but also has certain features of scripts in group C. There are other idiosyncrasies on this leaf also found on no. 26, such as the drooping tail of the final form of the letter *mim* and the thin, spike-like extensions to the final form of many letters.

The leaf is also remarkable for the colourful marginal illumination. This includes a *sajdah* (prostration) marker in the form of a roundel with three lines of white Kufic on alternately red, brown and blue grounds. Below this, *hizb* and tenth verse divisions have been marked with text in alternating blue, red, green and brown inks. Text in alternating colours is also a feature of nos. 23 and 29, both of which also make use of certain orthographic features that have been linked to the Maghrib and the Western Mediterranean (Blair 2006, p. 122; and nos. 14, 23, 26, 29). The coincidence of text in alternating colours with these features may suggest that it too is an indication of a western Islamic origin. In the top right corner of the verso the word *hubs*, the western Islamic word for a pious endowment, has been inscribed with pinpricks.

Two bifolia, containing marginal roundels with text in coloured inks, possibly from the same manuscript, were sold at Christie's, 7 April 2011, lot 18, and 20 April 1999, lot 303.

Though manuscripts in Déroche's group D.Va are typically small in size and horizontal in format, there are a few examples, such as this leaf, in a vertical format. Both this and the modern system of vocalization and reading marks look forward to manuscripts in Eastern Kufic script (e.g. nos. 43, 44). For other manuscripts in this script in a vertical format, see a section in the Museum of Turkish and Islamic Arts, Istanbul (Istanbul 2010a, no. 39), and two folios from the Nasser D. Khalili Collection (Déroche 1992, no. 50).

The leaf that would have followed this one in the original manuscript was published by Bernard Quaritch Ltd (Stanley 1995, no. 15). A bifolium from the same manuscript is in the Musée du Bardo, Tunis (Paris 1982, no. 338).

35

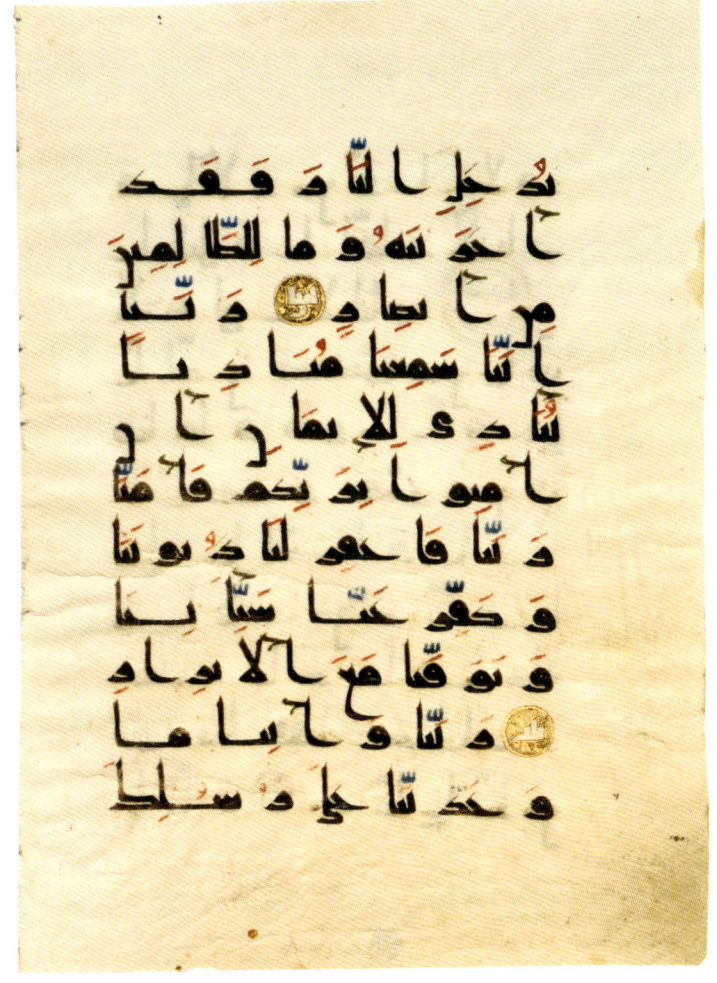

36

37
Leaf in Kufic script
Near East or North Africa
10th century CE
Surah 28 (*al-Qasas*), vv. 57–58

Folio from an Arabic manuscript on parchment, six lines of dark brown Kufic script per page; vocalization in form of red dots; letter-pointing in form of brown dashes; *hamzat al-qat'* marked with dark green dot; individual verse division marked with gold rosette with green centre pointed in red

17.9 × 13 cm

This folio is in a script classified by François Déroche as D.Vb (Déroche 1992, pp. 44–45). It shares some features with the D.Vc group (see nos. 39, 40), especially the vertical emphasis of the letters *alif* and *lam*. It does not, however, have the distinctive, deeply curving *nun* of that script, or the trailing tail of the letter *mim*. Manuscripts in this script were frequently, though not always (see e.g. no. 38), in a vertical format. For other examples in a vertical format, see Déroche 1992, nos. 56–57.

Another leaf from this manuscript is in the Beit al-Qur'an, Bahrain (Bahrain 1996, p. 80).

38
Leaf in Kufic script
Near East or North Africa
10th century CE
Surah 5 (*al-Ma'idah*), vv. 19–21

Folio from an Arabic manuscript on parchment, five lines of dark brown Kufic script per page; single verse divisions in form of an illuminated roundel inscribed with the word *ayah* (verse); tenth verse divisions in form of an elaborate illuminated roundel with the word *'ashar* (ten); vocalization in form of red dots; gold *shaddah* and green *hamzah* in their modern forms; signs marking long *alifs* in form of three green, gold and blue dashes

11.2 × 18.2 cm

The predominance of 'Eastern Kufic' or 'New Style' scripts is presaged in this leaf in François Déroche's style D.Vb by the graceful sway of the *lam-alif* letter combination.

An unusual feature is the use of three different colours for the three dashes marking long *alifs*. Like no. 36, this leaf is an early example of the use of the modern symbols for *shaddah* and *hamzah*. Though standard on Eastern Kufic and cursive scripts (see e.g. nos. 43, 44), these were unusual on Kufic manuscripts.

The script can be compared with that on another manuscript, three leaves from which are in the Tareq Rajab Museum, Kuwait (Safwat 1997, no. 34), and another in the Nasser D. Khalili Collection (Déroche 1992, no. 57).

37

38

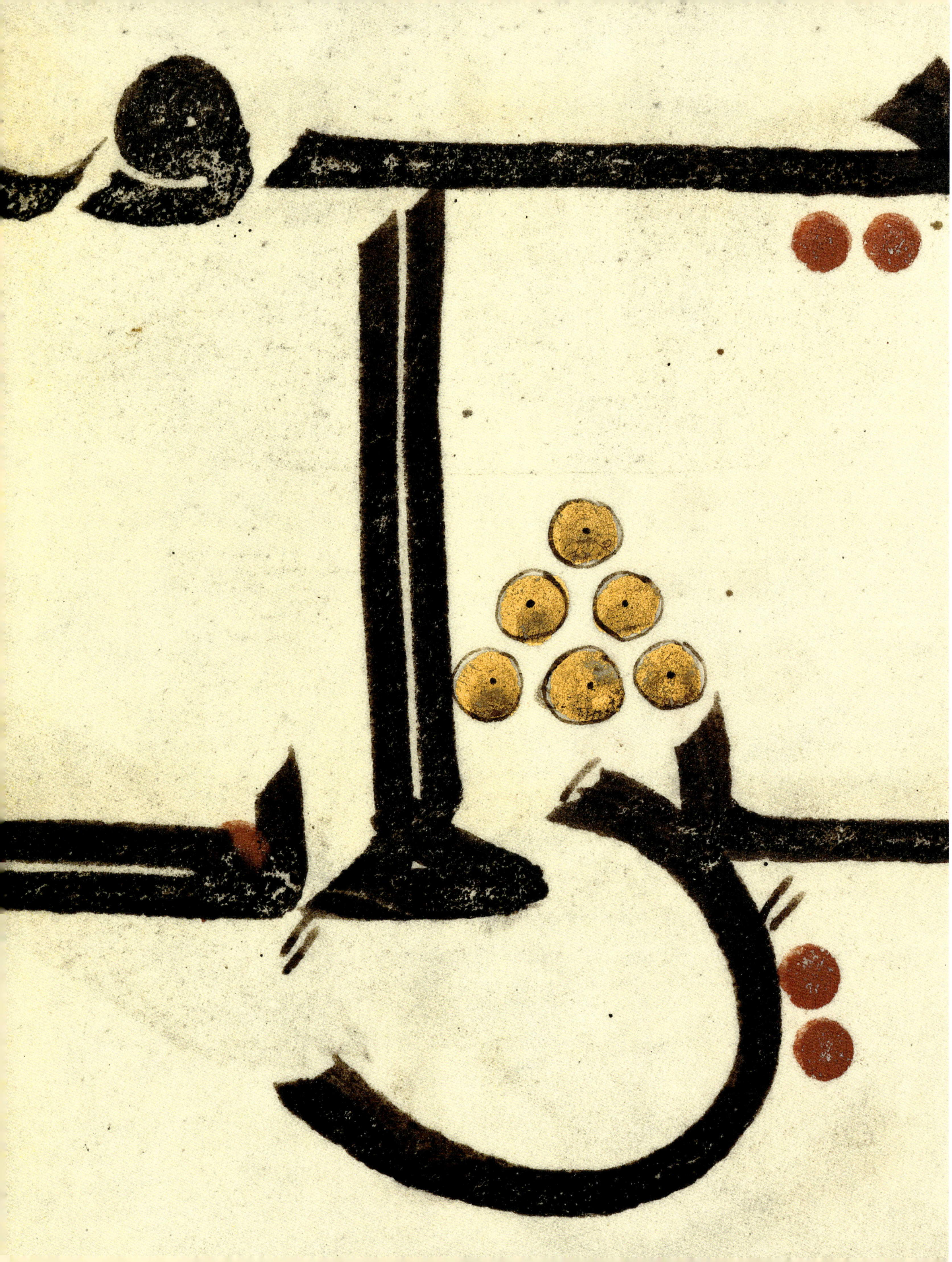

39
Large leaf in Kufic script
North Africa or Near East
1st half 10th century CE
Surah 56 (*al-Waqi'ah*), vv. 13–19

Folio from an Arabic manuscript on parchment, three lines of brown Kufic script per page; letter-pointing in from of sepia diagonal dashes; vocalization in form of red and yellow dots; *hamzat al-qat'* in form of green dots; individual verse divisions markers marked with triangular clusters of seven gold dots; tenth verse division marked with illuminated medallion with the word *'ashrun* (twenty) in reserve

23.8 × 33 cm

This beautiful leaf originates from a group of three luxury Qur'an manuscripts that share a distinctive style of Kufic script. Characteristics of the script are the oversized and emphatically rounded terminal *nun*, the thin, trailing tail of the terminal *mim*, and the slender, stretched verticals of the letters *lam* and *alif*. Certain features such as the trailing *mim* and the crooked vertical of the letter *ta/za* anticipate the predominance of New Style or Eastern Kufic scripts in the eleventh century. François Déroche has classified this script as D.Vc (Déroche 1992, pp. 42–45).

Though the manuscripts are now dispersed, it seems likely that they were produced by the same scriptorium, or may even have been the work of a single calligrapher. Fragments from the group are found in pre-modern collections in Damascus, Cairo and Qayrawan, and Déroche has linked the style to a *waqf* (endowment) inscription from Damascus dated 298 / 911 (Déroche 1992, pp. 44–45). This date, coupled with the stylistic nature of an essentially Kufic script that looks forward to the development of Eastern Kufic, would suggest a date in the tenth century.

The other manuscripts in the group are a dispersed seven-line Qur'an (see no. 40) and a five-line Qur'an of which a fragment of fifty-three folios is in the Bibliothèque nationale, Paris (Déroche 1983, no. 179).

Other leaves from the present manuscript are in the Al-Sabah Collection, Dar al-Athar al-Islamiyya, Kuwait

39 Detail

(New York 1992, fig. 1); the Tareq Rajab Museum, Kuwait (Safwat 1997, p. 35); the Aga Khan Museum (Paris 2007, no. 37); and the Nasser D. Khalili Collection (Déroche 1992, no. 58). A folio from the manuscript was exhibited in the Museum für Islamische Kunst, Berlin, in 2006 (Fraser and Kwiatkowski 2006, no. 14).

علمو ا
ا وا
من

فجاءوا الا ابا سلمه
وخلفاء سمعوا العدو الى الرسول
باموا و قد فشوا
و خطابا من الضعفوا
و الاسعا القصوا من اوسط
البلوا فضعفوا العولم الذين
ابا مهم باموا فشوا فاخفهم

40
Leaf in Kufic script
Near East or North Africa
10th century CE
Surah 21 (*al-Anbiya'*), vv. 68–77

Folio from an Arabic manuscript on parchment, seven lines of brown Kufic script per page; some original letter-pointing in form of thin dashes and some later letter-pointing, applied in a paler brown ink and coarser hand; vocalization in form of red and green dots; single verse divisions are marked with triangular clusters of six gold dots; a fifth verse division is marked with a large stylized letter *ha* in gold Kufic script; tenth verse divisions are marked with large illuminated rosettes decorated in gold and green and containing the exact verse count in gold Kufic script

33 × 46.2 cm

This large and refined Qur'an leaf comes from the same group of three manuscripts in a distinctive Kufic script as no. 39. Characteristics of the script are the oversized and emphatically rounded terminal *nun*, the thin, trailing tail of the terminal *mim*, and the slender, stretched verticals of the letters *lam* and *alif*.

Other folios and fragments from the same manuscript are in the Bibliothèque nationale, Tunis, and the Musée des Arts Islamiques, Qayrawan (Lings and Safadi 1976, no. 24; Paris 1982, no. 358). A leaf from the manuscript was exhibited in the Museum für Islamische Kunst, Berlin, in 2006 (Fraser and Kwiatkowski 2006, no. 13).

41
Bifolium in Eastern Kufic script
Near East
10th century CE
Surah 29 (*al-'Ankabut*), v. 66 – Surah 30 (*al-Rum*), v. 21
Surah 32 (*al-Sajdah*), v. 9 – Surah 33 (*al-Ahzab*), v. 2

Bifolium from an Arabic manuscript on parchment, fifteen lines of brown Eastern Kufic script per page; vocalization in form of red dots; occasional letter-pointing in brown ink; tenth verse markers in form of triangular clusters of three brown circle outlined in red

15 × 21 cm

This leaf is an early example of the 'Eastern Kufic' or 'New Style' script that began to displace traditional 'Abbasid Kufic scripts in the tenth century. Many of the letter forms have already begun to take on features of the 'New Style', such as the closed triangular shape of the medial form of the letter *'ayn*, the slight wave to some of the *alif* and *lam* letters, the rightward incline of the upper shaft of the letter *ṭa/ẓa* and the deep curve of the letter *nun*. However, the experimentation with these forms is inconsistent and tentative, suggesting an early stage in this development. This can be seen by comparing the leaf to a folio, also on parchment and of a smaller horizontal format on which these features are more pronounced, in the Nasser D. Khalili Collection (see Déroche 1992, no. 76). The present leaf does not use the contrast of thick and thin ligatures seen in more developed New Style scripts and retains something of the spirit of earlier Kufic leaves. This is visible in the relatively even thickness of the letter forms and some of the initial *alifs*, which retain a straight shape with an upward curve at the base (see Déroche 1992, nos. 55, 68).

42
Leaf in Kufic script
Near East or North Africa
10th century CE
Surah 3 (*Al 'Imran*), vv. 9–41

Folio from an Arabic manuscript on parchment, seventeen lines of brown Kufic script per page; no original vocalization or letter-pointing; verse divisions marked with vertical rows of short brown dashes; tenth verse divisions marked with simple red circles

14.8 × 21.5 cm

The script on this unusual Qur'an leaf shows many signs of the influence of cursive scripts. Particularly noticeable are the closed form of the letter *'ayn* as opposed to the open 'v' shape of Kufic scripts, and the final *mim* which sometimes ends in a tiny downward sloping stroke or with a long tail. The influence of cursive scripts on Kufic pages is generally associated with the tenth century and the experimentation with Qur'ans in Eastern Kufic or New Style script. This Qur'an leaf, however, does not display the typical features associated with Eastern Kufic, such as a high degree of angularity and a heightened contrast between the thin and thick parts of the letters (Déroche 1992, pp. 132–37).

The high word count to each page and the almost complete lack of ornamentation would suggest that the Qur'an was a working rather than a presentation copy. This may in part explain the idiosyncratic script, as the scribe may have been more versatile and felt freer than a scribe working strictly within the classical Qur'anic tradition.

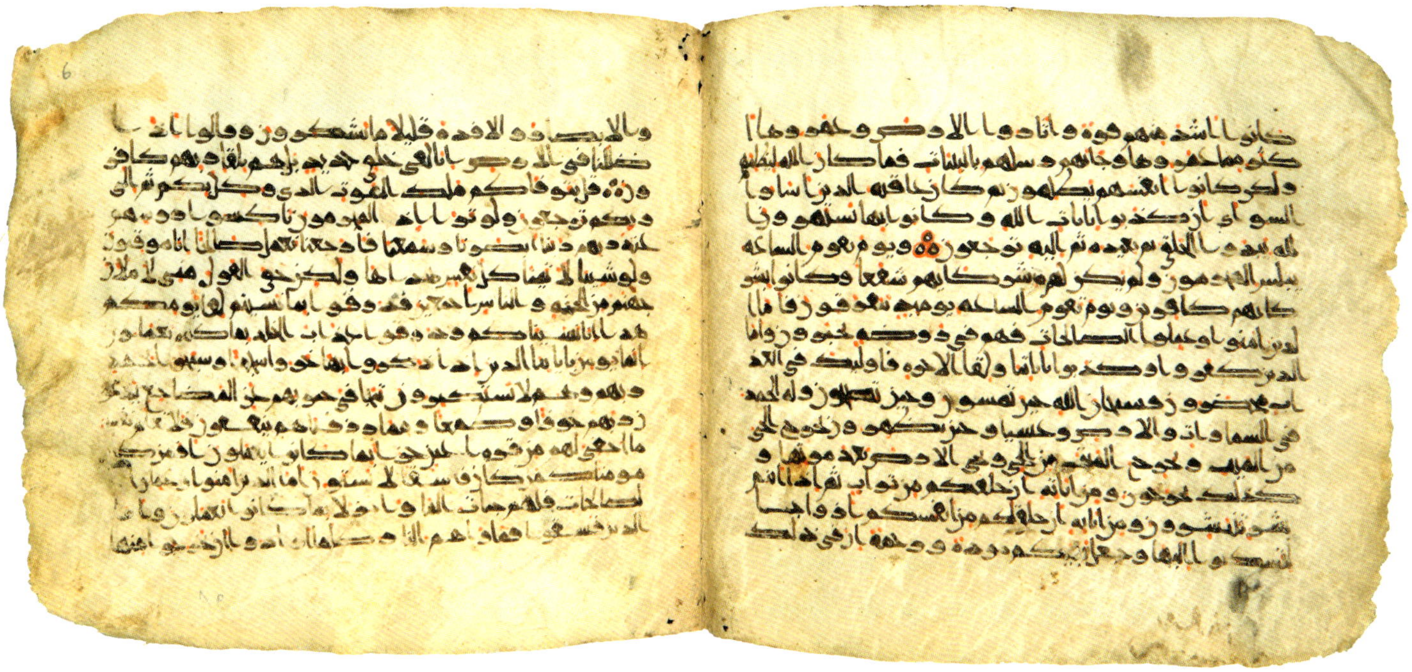

41

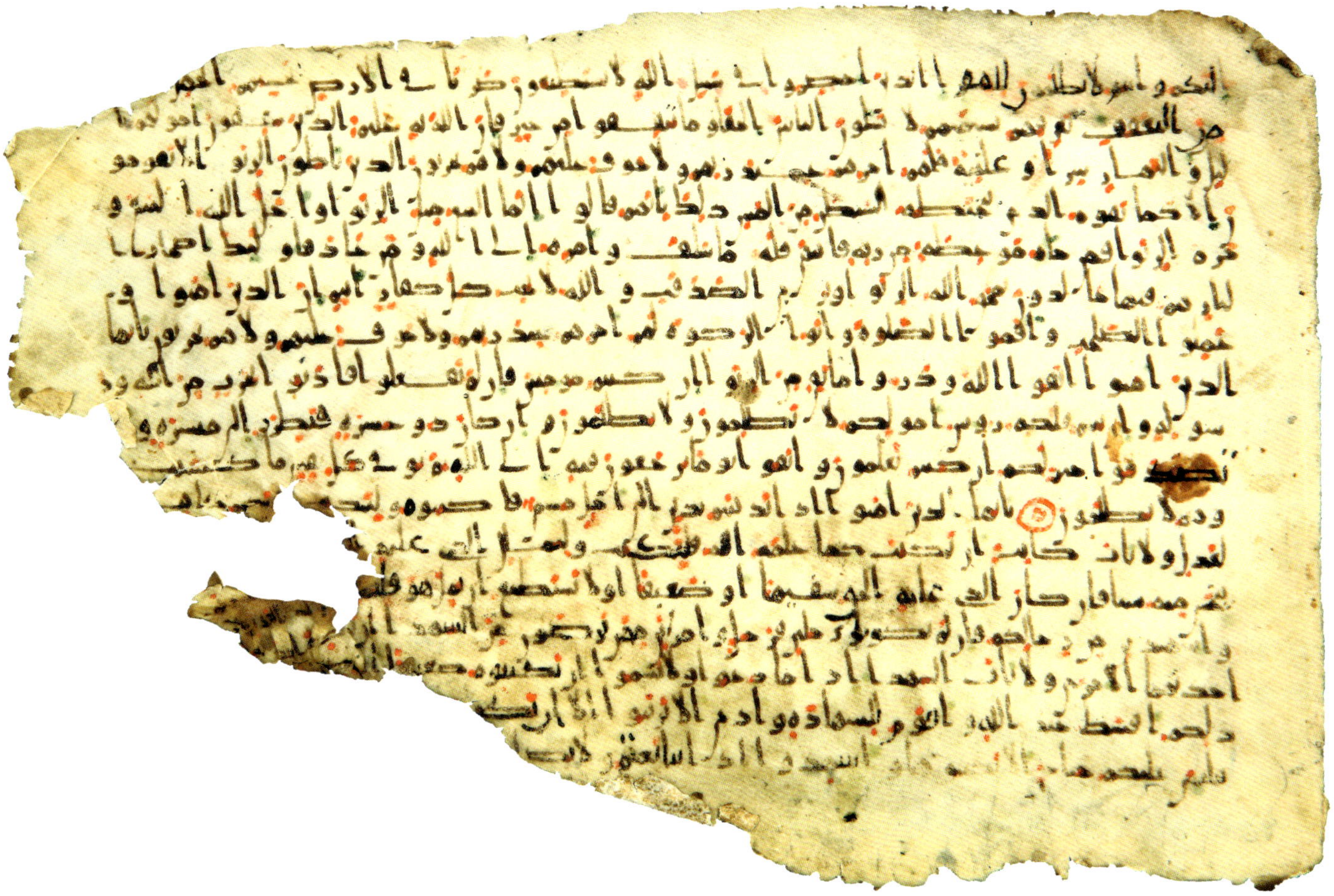

42

43
Bifolium in Eastern Kufic script
North Africa or Western Mediterranean
Late 10th century CE

Surah 99 (*al-Zalzalah*), v. 2 – Surah 100 (*al-'Adiyat*), v. 6
Surah 103 (*al-'Asr*), v. 2 – Surah 104 (*al-Humazah*), v. 9 and *surah* heading only of Surah 105 (*al-Fil*)

Bifolium from an Arabic manuscript on vellum, seven lines of Eastern Kufic script in black ink per page; partial use of letter-pointing; vocalization in red; fifth verse divisions marked with a stylized Kufic letter *ha*; headings written in gold Eastern Kufic script and with a stylized palmette extending into the margin

12.6 × 9.5 cm

This bifolium is probably an early example of the use of so-called 'New Style' or 'Eastern Kufic' script in the Maghrib or Western Mediterranean region around the late tenth century CE. We know that Eastern Kufic script was used in this region for Qur'ans in the late tenth century from a parchment manuscript copied at Palermo in Sicily in 982–83, fragments of which are now in the Nuruosmaniye Library, Istanbul (Ms. 23), and the Nasser D. Khalili Collection (Déroche 1992, no. 81). Qur'ans in Eastern Kufic and cursive scripts in Iran and Iraq from the same period on the other hand were already being copied on paper.

The calligraphic style of the present example is a fairly standard Eastern Kufic type, termed NS.I by Déroche (Déroche 1992, pp. 136–37). An unusual aspect of the script, however, is that it largely lacks letter-pointing, with only twelve instances across the four pages. It is unlikely that the manuscript was left incomplete as the vocalization, normally applied after the letter-pointing, appears in full. This phenomenon has been noted in relation to Kufic scripts of the late ninth century (Fraser and Kwiatkowski 2006, nos. 7, 8).

The size of this Qur'an is small even alongside other diminutive Eastern Kufic Qur'ans. Such volumes were perhaps intended to be portable for travel. The closest comparable manuscript in terms of size, calligraphy and illumination is a *juz'* in the Nasser D. Khalili Collection (see Déroche 1992, no. 80, pp. 144–145). Another similar example is in the Bibliothèque nationale, Tunis (Paris 1983, no. 360).

Another leaf from the same manuscript was sold at Sotheby's, 14 October 1999, lot 1.

بسم الله الرحمن الرحيم

والعاديات ضبحا
فالموريات قدحا
فالمغيرات صبحا
فأثرن به نقعا
فوسطن به جمعا ان الا
نسان لربه لكنود وانه

على ذلك لشهيد وانه
لحب الخير لشديد افلا يعلم اذا
بعثر ما في القبور وحصل ما
في الصدور ان ربهم بهم يومئذ
لخبير

بسم الله الرحمن الرحيم
القارعة ما القارعة
وما ادراك ما القارعة

44
Bifolium from the Nurse's Qur'an
Qayrawan, Tunisia
1019–20 CE
Surah 2 (*al-Baqarah*), vv. 171–175

Bifolium from an Arabic manuscript on parchment, five lines of brown Eastern Kufic per page; vocalization in red; modern forms of *shaddah* and *sukun* in blue, *hamzah* and in green

45 × 30 cm

This monumental parchment bifolium comes from one of the most celebrated medieval Islamic manuscripts ever produced, and one of the very few early Islamic manuscripts of which we know the date and circumstances of production. The manuscript was commissioned in 410 / 1019–20 by the Zirid emir of Ifriqiyyah (modern Tunisia), al-Mu'izz b. Badis. He supposedly presented the manuscript to his nurse, who in turn donated it to the Great Mosque of Qayrawan. The manuscript is frequently referred to as the 'Nurse's Qur'an'.

The script of this manuscript is distinctive and stylistically extreme. It has been termed 'Western Kufic' in the past (e.g. Lings and Safadi 1976, p. 30; Safadi 1978, p. 23), with reference to its origin, but there is no doubt that the script is an early and large example of Eastern Kufic or New Style script, the earliest dated example of which is a Qur'an manuscript made in Palermo in 982–83 CE (Déroche 1992, no. 8). Whereas the script in the Palermo manuscript is small and compact, however, the script in the Nurse's Qur'an is monumental and extravagant in its use of calligraphic flourishes. That it was copied on parchment indicates the relative conservatism of the Muslim west in matters of Qur'an production. In Iraq and Iran, by the early eleventh century, Qur'ans in Eastern Kufic script were frequently copied on paper (see e.g. no. 46).

Written on large, vertical parchment folios, with only five lines of script per page and an average of three words to each line, the manuscript must have been extremely costly in terms of materials and labour. As the Zirid emirate was no more than a hereditary dynasty of governors paying allegiance to the Fatimid caliph, one is led to wonder what degree of sophistication and monumentality caliphal commissions of the period may have been like.

Bifolia from the same manuscript are in the Nasser D. Khalili Collection (Amsterdam 1999, no. 56) and the David Collection, Copenhagen (inv. no. 25/2003). Other bifolia have been exhibited in the Museum of Fine Arts, Houston (Roxburgh 2008, fig. 12), and the Museum für Islamische Kunst, Berlin (Fraser and Kwiatkowski 2006, no. 15). Others again are in the Ibrahim ibn al-Aghlab Museum and the Musée des arts Islamiques, Qayrawan, and the Musée du Bardo, Tunis (see Lings 1978, no. 10; Paris 1982, nos. 356–57; and Lings and Safadi 1976, no. 25).

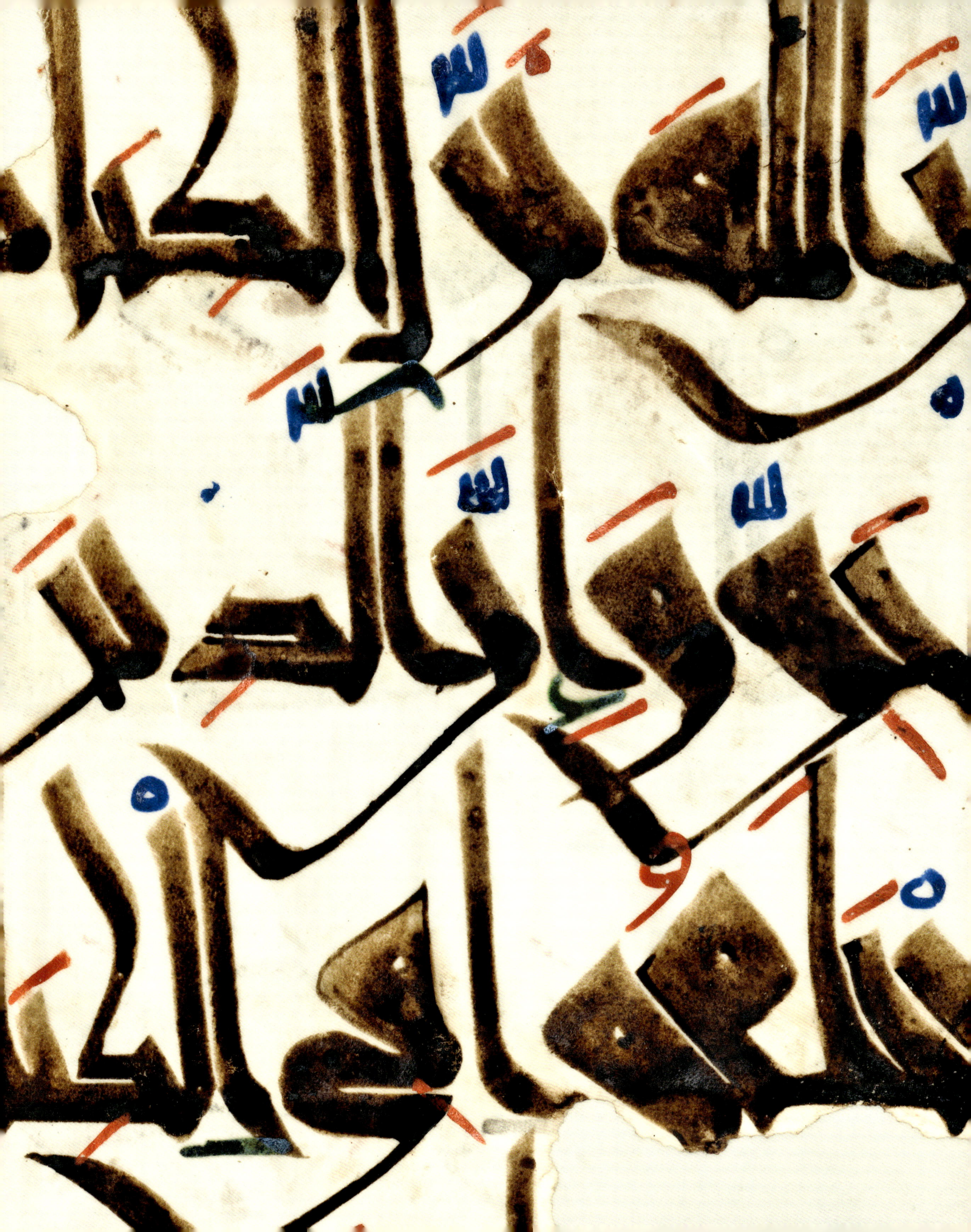

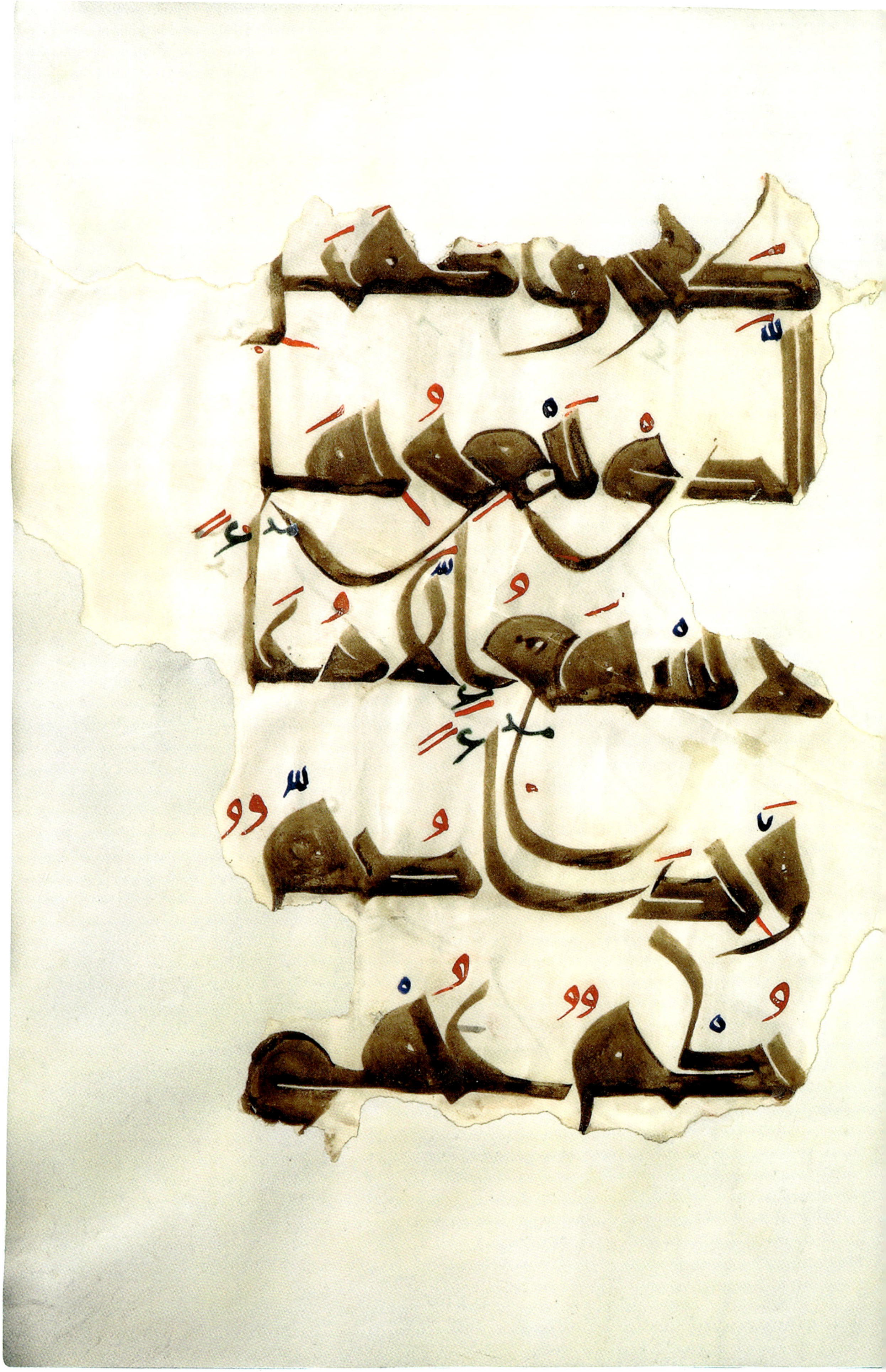

والعاديات
بابسم الله الرحمن الرحيم
والعاديات والنازعات
فالملغيات والناشطات
فوسعا فعده

45
Leaf in Maghribi script
Spain or North Africa
Early 11th century CE
Surah 25 (*al-Furqan*), v. 73 – Surah 26 (*al-Shu'ara*), v. 4

Folio from an Arabic manuscript on parchment, six lines of brown Maghribi script per page; *surah* heading in gold Kufic script with ornamental palmette projecting into the margin; the word *hubs* (endowment) has been written in brown ink at the top of the page

18.9 × 28.7 cm

This leaf comes from a very small group of early Maghribi Qur'ans written in horizontal format. Its script and format bear comparison to two leaves from a Qur'an in the Museum of Turkish and Islamic Art, Istanbul, which are the earliest dated example of a Qur'an in an identifiably Maghribi script. One of these leaves bears a colophon for the completion of a *juz'* in 398 / 1008, while the other gives the date of 432 / 1040 for the completion of the entire manuscript (Blair 2006, pp. 223–24). A two-volume Qur'an dated 393 / 1002–03, now in the Tareq Rajab Museum, Kuwait, is also in a script that has been called Maghribi, though is still clearly of an 'Abbasid Kufic type (Safwat 1997, pp. 36–37).

The horizontal format of the leaf is indicative of a transitional stage between the earlier tradition of horizontal Kufic manuscripts and the later, classical tradition of Maghribi manuscripts in upright (see nos. 53, 55, 57) or square (see nos. 54, 56) format. The type of Kufic script used for the *surah* heading is also that used on earlier Kufic Qur'ans rather than the more ornamental Kufic frequently used on later Maghribi manuscripts.

46
Folio in Eastern Kufic script
Near East
11th – 12th century CE
Surah 37 (*al-Saffat*), vv. 143–182 and *surah* heading and *basmalah* only of Surah 38 (*Sad*)

Folio from an Arabic manuscript on paper, between nineteen and twenty-one lines of black Eastern Kufic script per page; vocalization in red and green; single verse divisions marked with gold roundels; tenth verse divisions marked in margins with large illuminated roundels; *surah* heading written in gold; *basmalah* written in larger, more elaborate Eastern Kufic script; recto with a gold plaited frame round the text area

28.1 × 18.6 cm

The script on this leaf shows the tendency of certain New Style scripts towards stylization (see also Déroche 1992, nos. 92, 93, 95). This is particularly evident in the *basmalah* preceding the *surah* at the bottom of the page, where the contrast between the thin and thick parts of the letter forms is taken to an extreme.

45

بسم الله الرحمن الرحيم

أتاك الكتاب المبين كسر بلد
الا يكونوا مؤمنين ان نشأ ننزل عليهم
من السماء آية فظلت أعناقهم لها

46

47
Folio in Eastern Kufic script
Iran or Central Asia
11th – 12th century CE
Surah 5 (*al-Ma'idah*), vv. 54–55

Folio from an Arabic manuscript on paper, four lines of black Eastern Kufic script per page; vocalization in red, blue and yellow; letter-pointing in black; text block framed with band of gold lobed motifs with half palmettes extending into the margins in upper and lower corners; ground decorated with floral and foliate scroll in brown ink; verse division marked with large gold roundel containing verse count in *abjad* letters; *waqf* inscription in gold cursive script in bottom right corner of text block

31.2 × 21.1 cm

This leaf comes from a manuscript that is considered one of the masterpieces of Qur'anic calligraphy and illumination. It has been estimated that the complete manuscript, in thirty volumes and with only four lines to the page, would have stretched over approximately 2,250 leaves (Saint Laurent 1989, p. 117). The text block of each page has been decorated with a floral and vegetal scrolling pattern, a practice that was normally reserved for frontispieces and title pages (see Lings 1976, pls. 11, 16, 17, 19).

The script makes use of a combination of contrasts – between the extremely stretched verticals and relatively compact horizontals of the letters; between the angularity of many of the letter forms and the curvilinear elegance of others, in particular the terminal *nun* and the *lam-alif* combination; and between the exaggeratedly attenuated and thick parts of the letters. It has also been noted that there is considerable variety in the shape of the letter forms, which in part seem to have been dictated by the space available in the line (Saint Laurent 1989, pp. 117–19).

Comparisons have been made between the script of this manuscript and those of various manuscripts dating between 466 / 1073 and 573 / 1177–78 (Saint Laurent 1989, p. 121). The background of vegetal and floriate scroll has been compared to those on Seljuk pottery from the early thirteenth century as well as to decoration on the Minaret of Jam, which was built in the second half of the twelfth century (see catalogue entry, Sotheby's, 6 April 2011, lot 15).

A number of pages from the Qur'an, all from the sixth *juz'*, are in European and American collections. These include, among others, pages in the Aga Khan Museum (Istanbul 2010b, no. 13); the David Collection, Copenhagen (Blair and Bloom 2006, no. 26); the Museum für Islamische Kunst, Berlin; the Metropolitan Museum of Art; the Freer Gallery of Art, Smithsonian Institution, Washington D.C.; and the Cleveland Museum of Art. A bound volume of eleven folios from the same *juz'* is also in the Chester Beatty Library, Dublin (Arberry 1967, no. 37). A whole volume of the manuscript is in the Topkapi Saray (see Saint Laurent 1989, pp. 115–16).

This leaf was in the collection of Stuart Cary Welch along with a second folio that Welch sold to Philip Hofer in 1961. That leaf, which is now in the David Collection, was sold at Sotheby's, 15 October 1997, lot 10. It is thought that Welch probably bought both leaves in the 1950s from Adrienne Minassian, from whom Welch acquired a large part of his calligraphic collection.

EXHIBITED

Calligraphy in the Arts of the Muslim World, The Asia Society, New York; the Cincinnati Art Museum; the Seattle Art Museum; the St Louis Art Museum, 1979–80

Line and Space: Calligraphies from Medieval Islam, Harvard Art Museums, Cambridge, 1984

PUBLISHED
Welch 1979, no. 13

ما تبقون يهوون ويموتون
الا على الموت اغرة كل
الكافرين جاهد وفسق
لا وي حاف وزله جهنم

48
Bifolium in *naskh* script
Near East
11th – 12th century CE
Surah 2 (*al-Baqarah*). vv. 217–20, vv. 228–29

Bifolium from an Arabic manuscript on paper, seven lines of black *naskh* script per page; vocalization and letter-pointing in black; individual verse divisions marked with gold rosettes pointed in red

31.4 × 19.9 cm

The large format and relatively few lines of text per page on this bifolium are unusual for Seljuk Qur'ans in *naskh* script, which were typically compact and textually dense. Also unusual is the extension of the vertical of the final form of the *alif* below the line, a feature found on some types of Eastern Kufic script (e.g. nos. 43, 49, 52).

49
Leaf in Eastern Kufic script
Iranian region
11th – 12th century CE
Surah 7 (*al-A'raf*), vv. 100–29

Folio from an Arabic manuscript on paper, ten lines of black Eastern Kufic script per page; interlinear Persian translation in red ink; vocalization in black; single verse divisions marked with gold roundels; fifth verse divisions marked with illuminated pear-shaped devices; tenth verse divisions marked in margins with large illuminated roundels containing the exact verse count written in white Eastern Kufic script

36.6 × 30.5 cm

The Eastern Kufic script on this large leaf has a distinctly cursive character. The text is accompanied by an interlinear Persian translation, which, though common in the thirteenth and fourteenth centuries (see nos. 63–66), was still relatively uncommon at this date.

Ten folios from this manuscript appeared at Christie's, 25 April 1995, lot 24.

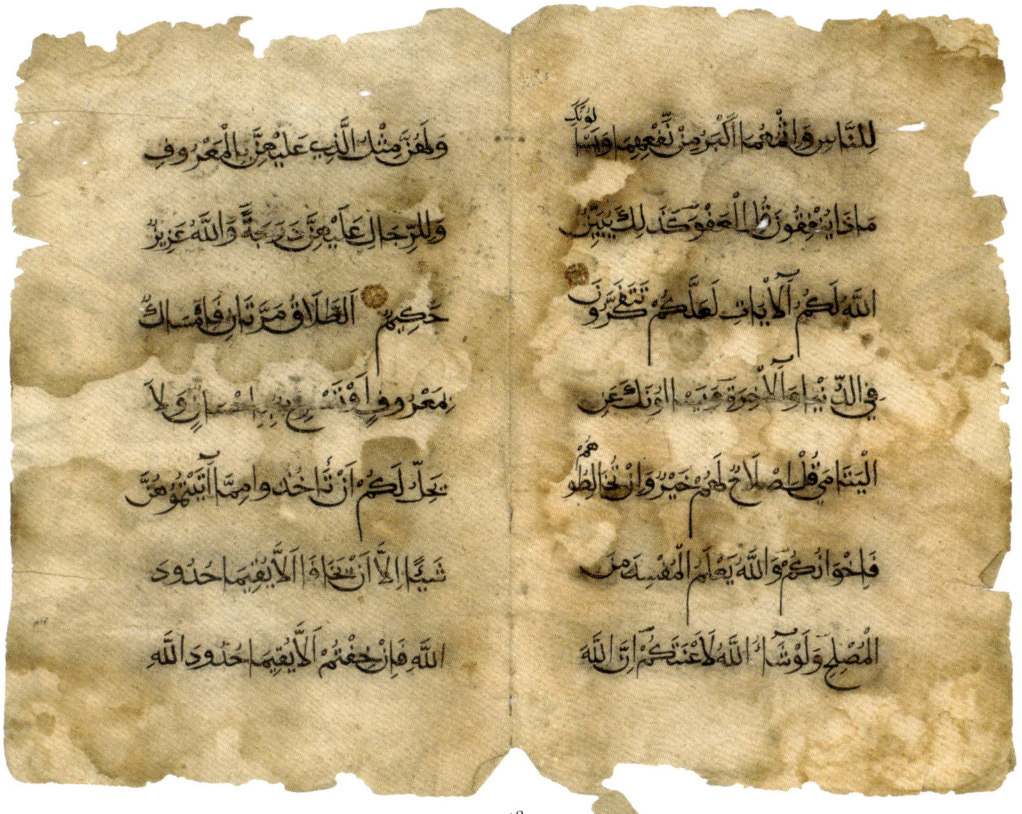

48

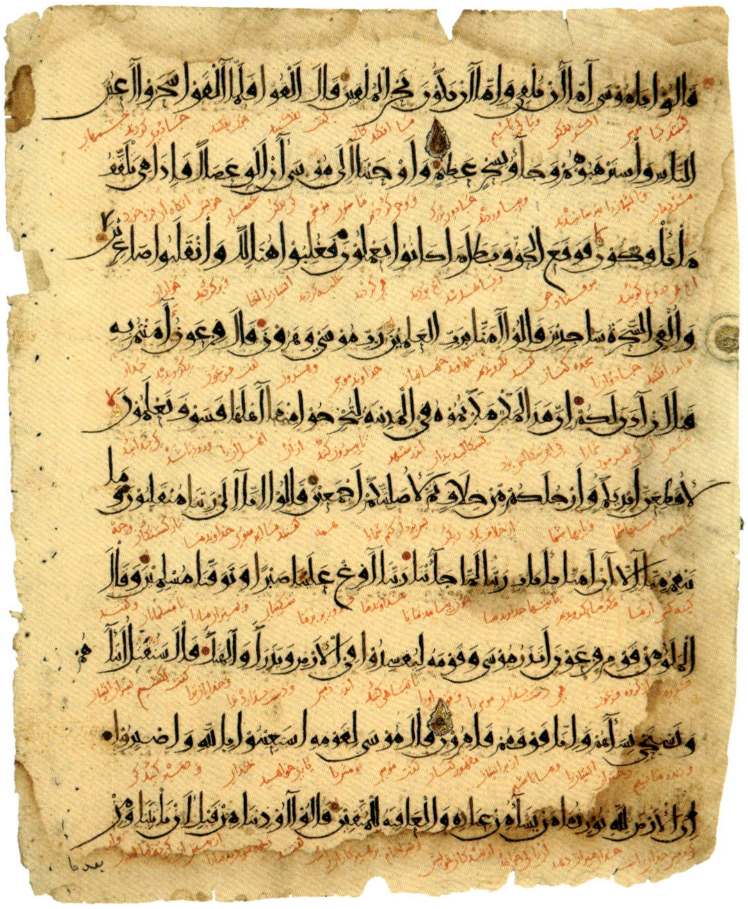

49

50
Leaf in Eastern Kufic script
Seljuk Anatolia or Iran
11th – 12th century CE
Surah 74 (*al-Muddaththir*), vv. 1–56 and illuminated heading of Surah 75 (*al-Qiyamah*)

Folio from an Arabic manuscript on dark buff paper, eleven to twelve lines of dark brown Eastern Kufic per page; vocalization in form of red dots; *shaddah* and *sukun* in green; individual verses marked in text with illuminated rosettes and teardrop devices, also marked in the margin with alternating roundels and palmettes; two *surah* headings of over 5–7 lines of smaller *naskh* script in red and black, within a gold band with gold palmette extending into the margin; marginal notes in red *naskh* on *qira'aat* under a green *qaf*

34 × 28 cm

This leaf in Eastern Kufic script is chiefly notable for the unusually detailed information given in the panels at the head of the *surahs*. This includes the number of the verses in the *surah* as well as the word and letter-count according to different sources. The *surah* panel on the recto (shown here) ends with a Prophetic tradition: 'Whoever reads this *surah*, Allah grants him ten rewards (*hasanat*) for good deeds'. This, and the notes on *qira'at* (correct readings) in the margin, suggest that this may have been a scholar's copy. The markers for *shaddah*, *sukun* and *hamzah* have been written in green ink and have assumed their modern shape.

Five leaves from the same manuscript were sold at Christie's, 11 April 2000, lot 3A.

51
Leaf in gold script
Near East
12th century CE
Surah 85 (*al-Buruj*), v. 5 – Surah 88 (*al-Ghashiyyah*), v. 14

Folio from an Arabic manuscript on paper, nineteen lines of gold *thulth* script outlined in black to the page; vocalization in red and blue; single verse divisions marked with small gold rosettes occasionally outlined in red ink; tenth verse divisions marked with large gold marginal medallions; *surah* headings in gold Kufic script on a red ground set in a rectangular cartouche with a lozenge-shaped ornament extending into the margins; the first *basmalah* of each *surah* is outlined in red ink

25 × 17 cm

This unusual leaf comes from a Qur'an written entirely in gold *thulth*. The rather crowded text has been compared to architectural inscriptions. Leaves from the same manuscript are in the Nasser D. Khalili Collection (James 1992a, no. 3; Abu Dhabi 2007, no. 62); the Beit al-Qur'an, Bahrain (Bahrain 1996, p. 87); and the Arab Museum for Modern Art, Doha (Doha 2006, no. 7).

50

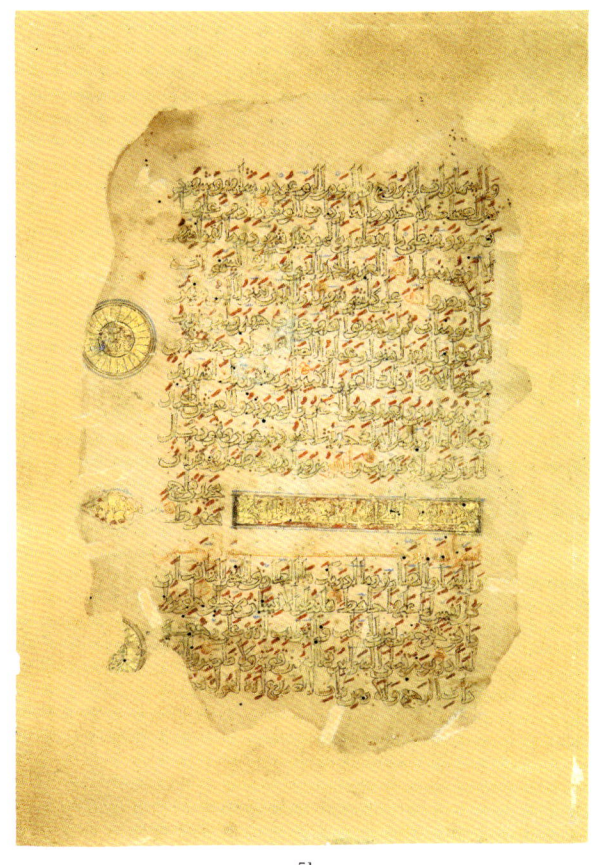

51

52
Section in Eastern Kufic script
Near East
12th century CE
Surah 2 (*al-Baqarah*), vv. 33–85

Arabic manuscript on dark buff paper, thirty folios with five lines of black Eastern Kufic script per page; vocalization and letter-pointing in black with additional markings in brown, red and blue; gold marginal medallions with verse count in *abjad* letters; reproduction binding incorporating part of a Mamluk binding

15.2 × 11 cm

By the twelfth century, when this Qur'an section was copied, horizontal manuscripts on parchment in traditional 'Abbasid Kufic scripts had been superseded by upright ones in *naskh* or New Style (Eastern Kufic) scripts on paper. These developments were certainly the result of the influence of secular and bureaucratic manuscript traditions, which had long employed this script and format.

The script is in a neat and unmannered New Style script. A Qur'an section in a similar script and of similar dimensions is in the Nasser D. Khalili Collection (see Déroche 1992, no. 88). Leaves from the same manuscript have appeared at Sotheby's, 24 April 1996, lot 5, and at Christie's, 1 May 2001, lot 13.

53 (*overleaf*)
Bifolium in Maghribi script on peach paper
Spain, probably Granada or Valencia
13th century CE
Surah 84 (*al-Inshiqaq*), vv. 14–22 and Surah 85 (*al-Buruj*), vv. 3–7

Bifolium from an Arabic manuscript on peach-coloured paper, five lines of brown Maghribi script per page; vocalization and letter-pointing in gold; *sukun* and *shaddah* in dark green; *hamzat al-qat'* and *hamzat al-wasl* marked with yellow and brown dots; single verse divisions marked with gold roundels containing the exact verse count according to the *abjad* system; fifth verse divisions marked with tear-shaped roundels with the words *khams* (five) in gold Kufic; inscription recording *hubs* (endowment) made with pin pricks in top right margin of verso

33.2 × 26 cm

The Qur'an from which this leaf originates was probably produced for a royal or noble patron in either Granada or Valencia (see New York 1992, no. 81). Though parchment was the standard material for Qur'an manuscripts in the west at this period, paper was occasionally used, particularly in the production of luxury copies. Another example, possibly from Tunisia and now in the Bibliothèque nationale, Paris, is in silver ink on chocolate paper (Paris 2001, no. 25).

Traditionally, this pink-coloured paper has been associated with Játiva (Shatiba), where high-quality paper was made that was exported all over the Mediterranean. While it is possible that it was made there before or after James I of Aragon's conquest of the city in 1244, it could also have been made in the Nasrid Kingdom of Granada, where coloured paper was used by the sultans for official correspondence (Bloom 2001, p. 88).

An unusual feature and an indication of the care and expense with which the manuscript was illuminated are the *abjad* letters in gold roundels giving the verse count for each verse. *Abjad* numerals were normally given only for tenth verse divisions.

A partially complete volume from the same manuscript is in the Bibliothèque Ben Youssouf, Marrakesh (New York 1992, no. 81). Further leaves are in, among other collections, the David Collection, Copenhagen (von Folsach 2001, no. 5), and the Aga Khan Museum (Geneva 1985, no. 7).

صفحة يمنى:
دوا يفعلون واد قتلتم
نفسا فادارتم فيها
والله مخرج ما كنتم
تكتمون فقلنا
اضربوه ببعضها

صفحة يسرى:
كذلك يحيي الله الموتى
ويريكم آياته
لعلكم تعقلون
ثم قست قلوبكم
من بعد ذلك فهي

إن الظن لا يغني
بلى إن ربه كان به
بصيرا ۝ فلا أقسم
بالشفق ۝ والليل وما
وسق ۝ والقمر إذا

بِالْمُؤْمِنِ سُمُوٓ
وَمَا نَقَمُوا مِنْهُمْ إِلَّا أَن
يُؤْمِنُوا بِاللَّهِ الْعَزِيزِ
الْحَمِيدِ الَّذِي لَهُ
مُلْكُ السَّمَوَتِ وَالْأَرْضِ

54
Leaf in Maghribi script
North Africa or Spain
13th – 14th century CE
Surah 2 (*al-Baqarah*), vv. 277–82

Folio from an Arabic manuscript on parchment, nine lines of brown Maghribi script per page; vocalization in red; *hamzat al-qat'* and *hamzat al-wasl* in form of yellow and green circles; *sukun* in form of blue circle; individual verses marked with gold roundels pointed in red and turquoise; fifth verse division marked in the margin with tear-shaped illuminated roundel containing the word *khams* (five) in Kufic script

18.6 × 16.5 cm

Multi-volume Qur'ans in large Maghribi script were popular in Spain and North Africa in the thirteenth and fourteenth centuries. It is thought that these Qur'ans, as opposed to the single-volume copies in a smaller hand that were also popular in the period, were associated with members of the Almohad and Marinid courts (Blair 2006, pp. 227–28). As in the case of this leaf, they were typically on parchment in square format and richly illuminated.

A section from the same manuscript was sold at Christie's, 13 April 2010, lot 54.

55
Leaf in Maghribi script
North Africa or Spain
13th – 14th century CE
Surah 5 (*al-Ma'idah*), vv. 36–38

Leaf from an Arabic manuscript on parchment, five lines of dark brown Maghribi script per page; vocalization in red; *hamzat al-wasl* marked with green dots, *hamzat al-qat'* with brown; *shaddah* and *sukun* in dark blue-green ink; individual verses marked with gold roundels pointed in red and blue containing the word *ayah* (verse)

26 × 20.3 cm

The tendency towards extension of the sublineal portions of the letters in Maghribi script is particularly evident on this leaf. A bifolium of similar dimensions and with corresponding illumination, probably from the same manuscript, is in the Arthur M. Sackler Museum, Harvard University Art Museums (Roxburgh 2008, fig. 14).

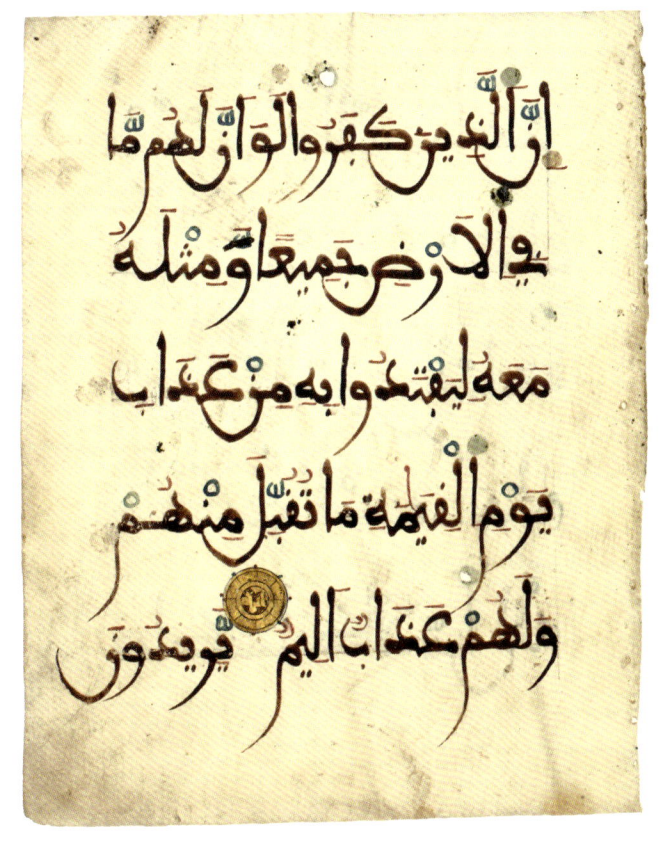

يمحق الله الربوا ويربي الصدقـ
ت والله لا يحب كل كفار أثيم
إن الذين ءامنوا وعملوا الصلحـ
ت وأقاموا الصلوة وءاتوا الزكوة
لهم أجرهم عند ربهم ولا خوف
عليهم ولا هم يحزنون يـأيـ
ها الذين ءامنوا اتقوا الله وذروا
ما بقي من الربوا إن كنتم مؤمنين
فإن لم تفعلوا فأذنوا بحرب

إن الذين كفروا لو أن لهم ما
في الأرض جميعا ومثله
معه ليفتدوا به من عذاب
يوم القيمة ما تقبل منهم
ولهم عذاب أليم يريدون

56
Leaf in Maghribi script
North Africa or Spain
13th – 14th century CE
Surah 7 (*al-A'raf*), v. 205 – Surah 8 (*al-Anfal*), v. 1

Folio from an Arabic manuscript on parchment, seven lines of brown Maghribi script per page; vocalization in red; *hamzat al-qat'* and *hamzat al-wasl* in form of yellow and green dots; individual verse divisions marked with gold trefoil device; fifth verse divisions marked with a gold *ha*-shaped device; *surah* heading consists of title and verse count in small gold ornamental Kufic on a blue ground within polygonal cartouches set in a panel of strapwork outlined in gold and gold vegetal scroll, with a gold palmette extending into the margin

19.7 × 19.7 cm

Unusually for a Maghribi Qur'an in square format, the *surah* title has here been placed in two geometric cartouches within an illuminated panel. Unless the beginning of a *surah* happened to coincide with the beginning of a *juz'* (for an example see Salameh 2001, no. 3, pp. 78–79), the *surah* title and verse count were normally left unframed.

Qur'ans in seven lines were popular in North Africa and Spain and were typically arranged in four volumes (James 1992a, nos. 55, 58).

57
Leaf in gold Maghribi script
Marinid Morocco or Nasrid Kingdom of Granada
13th – 14th century CE
Surah 10 (*Yunus*), vv. 59–63

Folio from an Arabic manuscript on parchment, nine lines of gold Maghribi script per page; vocalization in red; *shaddah* and *sukun* marked in blue; *hamzat al-qat'* and *hamzat al-wasl* marked with yellow and green dots; individual verse divisions marked with an illuminated roundel containing the word *ayah* (verse) reserved in Kufic script on a blue ground

19.5 × 17 cm

This impressive folio comes from one of only two Qur'ans in Maghribi script in which the entire text is written in original gold. The other is a manuscript in the John Rylands Library, Manchester University (ms. 18). The script of the present folio is of a large, looping type, with letter-pointing also in gold, and the manuscript must formerly have been bound in several volumes. This would perhaps indicate an original function in a mosque or royal library. It has been suggested by David James that this Qur'an was made for a caliph or king in Granada or Morocco (James 1992a, p. 214).

Other sections and leaves from the same manuscript are in the Topkapi Saray Library, Istanbul; the Chester Beatty Library, Dublin; Eton College Library, Windsor; Bibliothèque nationale, Paris; the Keir Collection, London; the Metropolitan Museum of Art, New York; the Aga Khan Museum; the National Library, Cairo; the Tareq Rajab Museum, Kuwait; and the Nasser D. Khalili Collection.

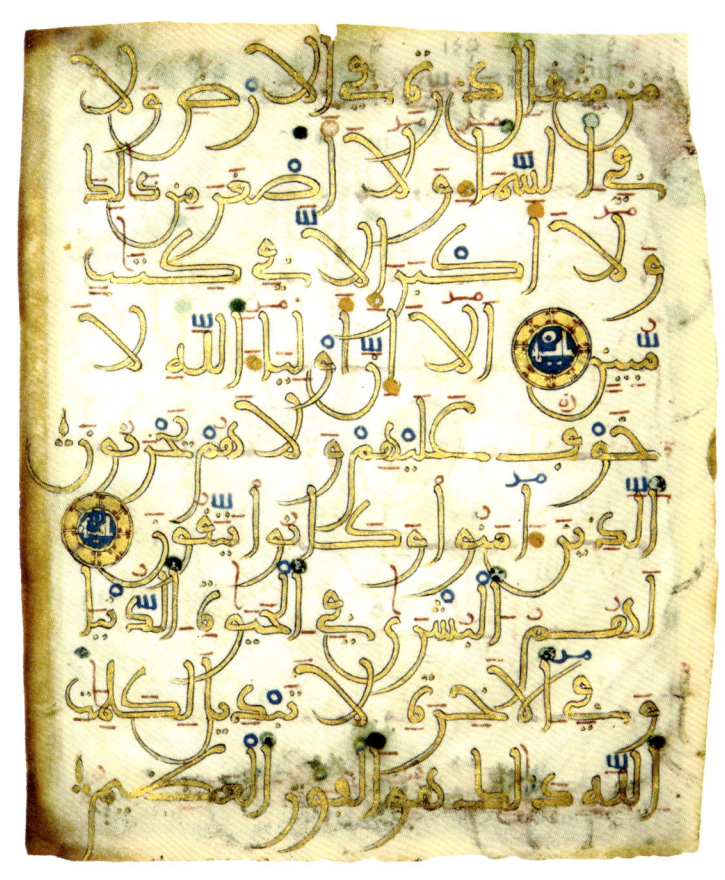

بسم الله الرحمن الرحيم
يسألونك عن الأنفال
قل الأنفال لله والرسول
فاتقوا الله وأصلحوا ذات
بينكم وأطيعوا الله

من مثقال ذرة في الأرض ولا
في السماء ولا أصغر من ذلك
ولا أكبر إلا في كتاب
مبين ألا إن أولياء الله لا
خوف عليهم ولا هم يحزنون
الذين آمنوا وكانوا يتقون
لهم البشرى في الحياة الدنيا
وفي الآخرة لا تبديل لكلمات
الله ذلك هو الفوز العظيم

58
Leaf in three scripts
Yemen or Iran
13th – 14th century CE
Surah 55 (*al-Rahman*), v. 71 – Surah 56 (*al-Waqi'ah*), v. 54

Folio from an Arabic manuscript on paper, twelve to thirteen lines of text per page, the first and last lines in large black *muhaqqaq* script outlined in gold, the central line in large gold *thulth* script outlined in black, remaining lines in black *naskh* script; individual verse divisions marked with gold rosettes; fifth verses marked in margins with gold pear-shaped medallion; tenth verses marked in the margins with gold roundels

39 × 31.1 cm

No origin has been securely established for the unusual manuscript from which this leaf came. The bulk of the text is in *naskh*, which was the standard script for Qur'ans in the Mamluk Empire until the first half of the fourteenth century. The use of three different scripts on the same page, however, has no precedent from that region (James 1992a, p. 160). The style of the illumination and the gold outlining of the monumental black *muhaqqaq* script may rather point to an Ilkhanid origin (Abu Dhabi 2008, p. 142). Undocumented sources have attributed the manuscript to Yemen in the Rasulid period (1229–1454 CE), which might explain why the manuscript has a superficially Mamluk appearance, yet clearly betrays the influence of other traditions (James 1992a, p. 142).

Two leaves from the manuscript are in the Nasser D. Khalili Collection (Abu Dhabi 2008, no. 165; James 1992a, no. 40). A further leaf is in the Aga Khan Museum (Istanbul 2010b, no. 29).

59
Leaf in *naskh* script
Mamluk Cairo, illumination attributed to Sandal
c. 1300–10 CE
Surah 96 (*al-'Alaq*), vv. 2–19 and heading and *basmalah* of Surah 97 (*al-Qadr*)

Folio from an Arabic manuscript on paper, six lines of black *naskh* script per page; individual verses marked with gold rosettes pointed in blue and red; fifth verses marked with gold tear-shaped marginal medallions; tenth verses marked with illuminated marginal roundels containing the word *'ashar* (ten) reserved in gold ornamental Kufic on a blue ground; *surah* heading in gold Eastern Kufic; heavily trimmed

19.4 × 14.2 cm

This Qur'an leaf comes from a small group of Qur'ans, including the Baybars al-Jashnagir Qur'an in the British Library, that can be attributed to the atelier of one of the master illuminators of Mamluk Cairo, Abu Bakr, known as 'Sandal'. Whereas the main text of Qur'ans was copied according to strict rules, there was great variation in the way in which the ornamental headings might be written. The *surah* heading in an elegant geometric ornamental Kufic on this leaf is almost identical to those in a Qur'an illuminated and signed by Sandal in the Chester Beatty Library (James 1988, no. 3).

58

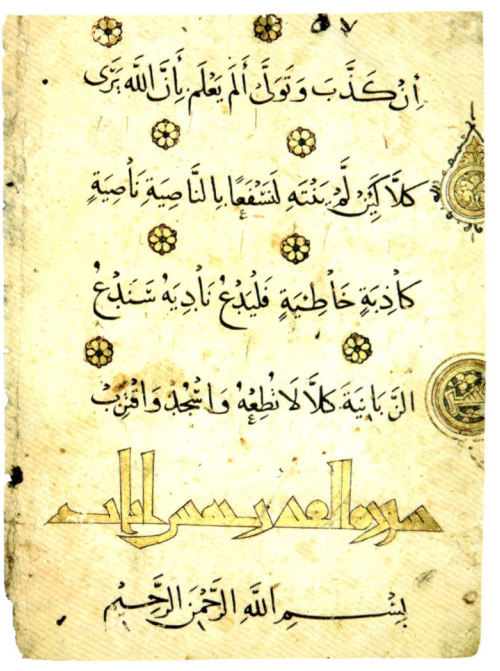

تُكَذِّبَانِ حُورٌ مَقْصُورَاتٌ
فِي الْخِيَامِ فَبِأَيِّ آلَاءِ رَبِّكُمَا تُكَذِّبَانِ لَمْ يَطْمِثْهُنَّ إِنْسٌ قَبْلَهُمْ وَلَا جَانٌّ فَبِأَيِّ
آلَاءِ رَبِّكُمَا تُكَذِّبَانِ مُتَّكِئِينَ عَلَىٰ رَفْرَفٍ خُضْرٍ وَعَبْقَرِيٍّ حِسَانٍ فَبِأَيِّ آلَاءِ
رَبِّكُمَا تُكَذِّبَانِ تَبَارَكَ اسْمُ رَبِّكَ ذِي الْجَلَالِ وَالْإِكْرَامِ

سورة الواقعة مكية وهي ستٌ وتسعون آية

بِسْمِ اللَّهِ الرَّحْمَٰنِ الرَّحِيمِ
إِذَا وَقَعَتِ الْوَاقِعَةُ لَيْسَ لِوَقْعَتِهَا كَاذِبَةٌ خَافِضَةٌ رَافِعَةٌ إِذَا رُجَّتِ
الْأَرْضُ رَجًّا وَبُسَّتِ الْجِبَالُ بَسًّا فَكَانَتْ هَبَاءً مُنْبَثًّا وَكُنْتُمْ أَزْوَاجًا
ثَلَاثَةً فَأَصْحَابُ الْمَيْمَنَةِ مَا أَصْحَابُ الْمَيْمَنَةِ وَأَصْحَابُ الْمَشْأَمَةِ مَا
أَصْحَابُ الْمَشْأَمَةِ وَالسَّابِقُونَ السَّابِقُونَ أُولَٰئِكَ الْمُقَرَّبُونَ فِي جَنَّاتِ النَّعِيمِ ثُلَّةٌ مِنَ الْأَوَّلِينَ
وَقَلِيلٌ مِنَ الْآخِرِينَ عَلَىٰ سُرُرٍ مَوْضُونَةٍ مُتَّكِئِينَ عَلَيْهَا مُتَقَابِلِينَ يَطُوفُ عَلَيْهِمْ وِلْدَانٌ

مُخَلَّدُونَ بِأَكْوَابٍ وَأَبَارِيقَ

59

أَنْ كَذَّبَ وَتَوَلَّىٰ أَلَمْ يَعْلَمْ بِأَنَّ اللَّهَ يَرَىٰ
كَلَّا لَئِنْ لَمْ يَنْتَهِ لَنَسْفَعًا بِالنَّاصِيَةِ نَاصِيَةٍ
كَاذِبَةٍ خَاطِئَةٍ فَلْيَدْعُ نَادِيَهُ سَنَدْعُ
الزَّبَانِيَةَ كَلَّا لَا تُطِعْهُ وَاسْجُدْ وَاقْتَرِبْ

سورة لم يكن

بِسْمِ اللَّهِ الرَّحْمَٰنِ الرَّحِيمِ

60
Leaf in *muhaqqaq* script
Mamluk Egypt
c. 1328 CE
Surah 11 (*Hud*), vv. 66–81

Folio from an Arabic manuscript on thick burnished soft pink paper, thirteen lines of black *muhaqqaq* script per page; individual verse divisions marked with gold and coloured rosettes; fifth verse endings marked with elaborate illuminated vase-shaped marginal ornaments containing the word *khams* (five); tenth verse endings marked with large illuminated circular marginal ornament containing the word *'ashar* (ten); *waqf* inscription on top of recto

44.8 × 33.3 cm

The manuscript from which this leaf comes is notable for its pinkish paper and colourful illumination, which shows signs of Ilkhanid influence. Large Qur'ans of this sort, with many lines of *muhaqqaq* script to the page, were popular in the Mamluk Empire in the fourteenth and fifteenth centuries. In terms of calligraphy and illumination, the manuscript has been linked to a group of Mamluk Qur'ans dated to the 1330s and 1340s (see Sotheby's, 6 April 2011, lot 16). A leaf from the manuscript, sold at Sotheby's, 21 April 2008, lot 21, had been previously published as coming from a manuscript copied by a certain 'Abdallah ibn Mansur Hashimi al-'Abbasi on 7 Sha'ban 728 / 17 June 1328, implying that the colophon from the manuscript was once known.

Other leaves from this manuscript are in the Aga Khan Museum (Istanbul 2010b, no. 28) and in the Medelhavsmuseet, Stockholm (inv. no. BekB-118). In addition to the ones mentioned above, a further leaf from this manuscript was sold at Sotheby's, 14 April 2010, lot 11.

61
Leaf in *muhaqqaq* script
Mamluk Egypt
14th century CE
Surah 39 (*al-Zumar*), vv. 1–23

Folio from an Arabic manuscript on paper, thirteen lines of black *naskh* script per page; individual verses marked with gold rosettes pointed in blue and red; fifth verse division marked with gold marginal roundel with blue outline and vertical extensions containing the word *khams* (five) in gold Kufic script

65.4 × 55.7 cm

Extremely large Qur'ans were popular among the Mamluk elite from the 1340s to the early fifteenth century. It has been suggested that their popularity may have been due to a desire to outstrip monumental Ilkhanid manuscripts, or may even have been an affirmation of the Mamluks' self-confidence after the collapse of the rival Ilkhanid Empire in the 1330s (Fraser and Kwiatkowski 2006, p. 102). For a Qur'an of similar dimensions and in a comparable *muhaqqaq* script, see a leaf in the Bibliothèque nationale (Paris 2001, no. 23).

بِسْمِ اللَّهِ الرَّحْمَٰنِ الرَّحِيمِ

تَنزِيلُ الْكِتَابِ مِنَ اللَّهِ الْعَزِيزِ الْحَكِيمِ إِنَّا أَنزَلْنَا إِلَيْكَ الْكِتَابَ بِالْحَقِّ فَاعْبُدِ اللَّهَ مُخْلِصًا لَّهُ الدِّينَ

أَلَا لِلَّهِ الدِّينُ الْخَالِصُ وَالَّذِينَ اتَّخَذُوا مِن دُونِهِ أَوْلِيَاءَ مَا نَعْبُدُهُمْ إِلَّا لِيُقَرِّبُونَا إِلَى اللَّهِ زُلْفَىٰ إِنَّ اللَّهَ يَحْكُمُ بَيْنَهُمْ

فِي مَا هُمْ فِيهِ يَخْتَلِفُونَ إِنَّ اللَّهَ لَا يَهْدِي مَنْ هُوَ كَاذِبٌ كَفَّارٌ لَّوْ أَرَادَ اللَّهُ أَن يَتَّخِذَ وَلَدًا لَّاصْطَفَىٰ

مِمَّا يَخْلُقُ مَا يَشَاءُ سُبْحَانَهُ هُوَ اللَّهُ الْوَاحِدُ الْقَهَّارُ خَلَقَ السَّمَاوَاتِ وَالْأَرْضَ بِالْحَقِّ يُكَوِّرُ اللَّيْلَ عَلَى

النَّهَارِ وَيُكَوِّرُ النَّهَارَ عَلَى اللَّيْلِ وَسَخَّرَ الشَّمْسَ وَالْقَمَرَ كُلٌّ يَجْرِي لِأَجَلٍ مُّسَمًّى أَلَا هُوَ الْعَزِيزُ الْغَفَّارُ

خَلَقَكُم مِّن نَّفْسٍ وَاحِدَةٍ ثُمَّ جَعَلَ مِنْهَا زَوْجَهَا وَأَنزَلَ لَكُم مِّنَ الْأَنْعَامِ ثَمَانِيَةَ أَزْوَاجٍ

يَخْلُقُكُمْ فِي بُطُونِ أُمَّهَاتِكُمْ خَلْقًا مِّن بَعْدِ خَلْقٍ فِي ظُلُمَاتٍ ثَلَاثٍ ذَٰلِكُمُ اللَّهُ رَبُّكُمْ

لَهُ الْمُلْكُ لَا إِلَٰهَ إِلَّا هُوَ فَأَنَّىٰ تُصْرَفُونَ إِن تَكْفُرُوا فَإِنَّ اللَّهَ غَنِيٌّ عَنكُمْ وَلَا يَرْضَىٰ لِعِبَادِهِ الْكُفْرَ

وَإِن تَشْكُرُوا يَرْضَهُ لَكُمْ وَلَا تَزِرُ وَازِرَةٌ وِزْرَ أُخْرَىٰ ثُمَّ إِلَىٰ رَبِّكُم مَّرْجِعُكُمْ فَيُنَبِّئُكُم

بِمَا كُنتُمْ تَعْمَلُونَ إِنَّهُ عَلِيمٌ بِذَاتِ الصُّدُورِ وَإِذَا مَسَّ الْإِنسَانَ ضُرٌّ دَعَا رَبَّهُ مُنِيبًا إِلَيْهِ ثُمَّ

إِذَا خَوَّلَهُ نِعْمَةً مِّنْهُ نَسِيَ مَا كَانَ يَدْعُو إِلَيْهِ مِن قَبْلُ وَجَعَلَ لِلَّهِ أَندَادًا لِّيُضِلَّ عَن سَبِيلِهِ

قُلْ تَمَتَّعْ بِكُفْرِكَ قَلِيلًا إِنَّكَ مِنْ أَصْحَابِ النَّارِ أَمَّنْ هُوَ قَانِتٌ آنَاءَ اللَّيْلِ سَاجِدًا وَقَائِمًا يَحْذَرُ الْآخِرَةَ

قَوْمِ لُوطٍ إِنَّ إِبْرَاهِيمَ لَحَلِيمٌ أَوَّاهٌ مُّنِيبٌ يَا إِبْرَاهِيمُ

أَعْرِضْ عَنْ هَٰذَا إِنَّهُ قَدْ جَاءَ أَمْرُ رَبِّكَ وَإِنَّهُمْ آتِيهِمْ عَذَابٌ

غَيْرُ مَرْدُودٍ وَلَمَّا جَاءَتْ رُسُلُنَا لُوطًا سِيءَ بِهِمْ وَضَاقَ

بِهِمْ ذَرْعًا وَقَالَ هَٰذَا يَوْمٌ عَصِيبٌ وَجَاءَهُ قَوْمُهُ

يُهْرَعُونَ إِلَيْهِ وَمِن قَبْلُ كَانُوا يَعْمَلُونَ

السَّيِّئَاتِ قَالَ يَا قَوْمِ هَٰؤُلَاءِ بَنَاتِي هُنَّ أَطْهَرُ لَكُمْ

فَاتَّقُوا اللَّهَ وَلَا تُخْزُونِ فِي ضَيْفِي أَلَيْسَ مِنكُمْ رَجُلٌ

رَّشِيدٌ قَالُوا لَقَدْ عَلِمْتَ مَا لَنَا فِي بَنَاتِكَ مِنْ حَقٍّ

وَإِنَّكَ لَتَعْلَمُ مَا نُرِيدُ قَالَ لَوْ أَنَّ لِي بِكُمْ قُوَّةً أَوْ

آوِي إِلَىٰ رُكْنٍ شَدِيدٍ قَالُوا يَا لُوطُ إِنَّا رُسُلُ

رَبِّكَ لَن يَصِلُوا إِلَيْكَ فَأَسْرِ بِأَهْلِكَ بِقِطْعٍ مِّنَ اللَّيْلِ

وَلَا يَلْتَفِتْ مِنكُمْ أَحَدٌ إِلَّا امْرَأَتَكَ إِنَّهُ مُصِيبُهَا مَا

أَصَابَهُمْ إِنَّ مَوْعِدَهُمُ الصُّبْحُ أَلَيْسَ الصُّبْحُ بِقَرِيبٍ

62
Bifolium from a Qur'an attributed to Arghun al-Kamili
Probably Baghdad
C. 1335 CE
Surah 39 (*al-Zumar*), vv. 32–45 and Surah 41 (*Fussilat/al-Sajdah*) vv. 1–15

Bifolium from an Arabic manuscript on paper, thirteen lines of black *rayhani* script per page; individual verses marked with gold rosettes pointed in dark blue; fifth verse divisions marked with marginal tear-shaped medallions with gold Kufic on a blue ground within a gold border; tenth verse divisions marked with round marginal medallions with gold Kufic on a blue ground within a gold border; surah heading in gold *thulth* outlined in black issuing a marginal device composed of blue leaves with gold edges; marginal medallion marking *juz'* division with white *thulth* on a blue ground within a geometric border; catchwords in bottom left corner of verso

37.7 × 55.5 cm

This bifolium comes from a celebrated Qur'an attributed to the master scribe Arghun al-Kamili. One of the six famous pupils of Yaqut al-Musta'simi, he was either Persian or Turkish in origin, but was brought up in Baghdad (James 1988, p. 157). The attribution of this Qur'an to Arghun al-Kamili has been made on the basis of similarities with four Qur'ans in the Chester Beatty Library, Dublin, all copied by him between 1329 and 1341. Like this manuscript, they are written in thirteen lines per page of beautiful *rayhani* script and illuminated in a style associated with the illuminator Muhammad ibn Sayf al-Din *al-Naqqash,* 'the Illuminator' (James 1988, pp. 158–60).

The bulk of the manuscript is in the Museum of Turkish and Islamic Arts, Istanbul. Further leaves include nineteen folios in the Chester Beatty Library, Dublin; twenty-eight leaves that were exhibited in Riyadh in 1985 (Riyadh 1985, no. 17); a bifolium published by Bernard Quaritch (Stanley 1995, no. 25); and a single leaf in the former Art and History Trust Collection (Soudavar 1992, no. 12). A bifolium was sold at Christie's, 26 April 1994, lot 36, and two single leaves were sold at Sotheby's, 14 April 2010, lots 9, 10.

...سورة أربع آيات مكية

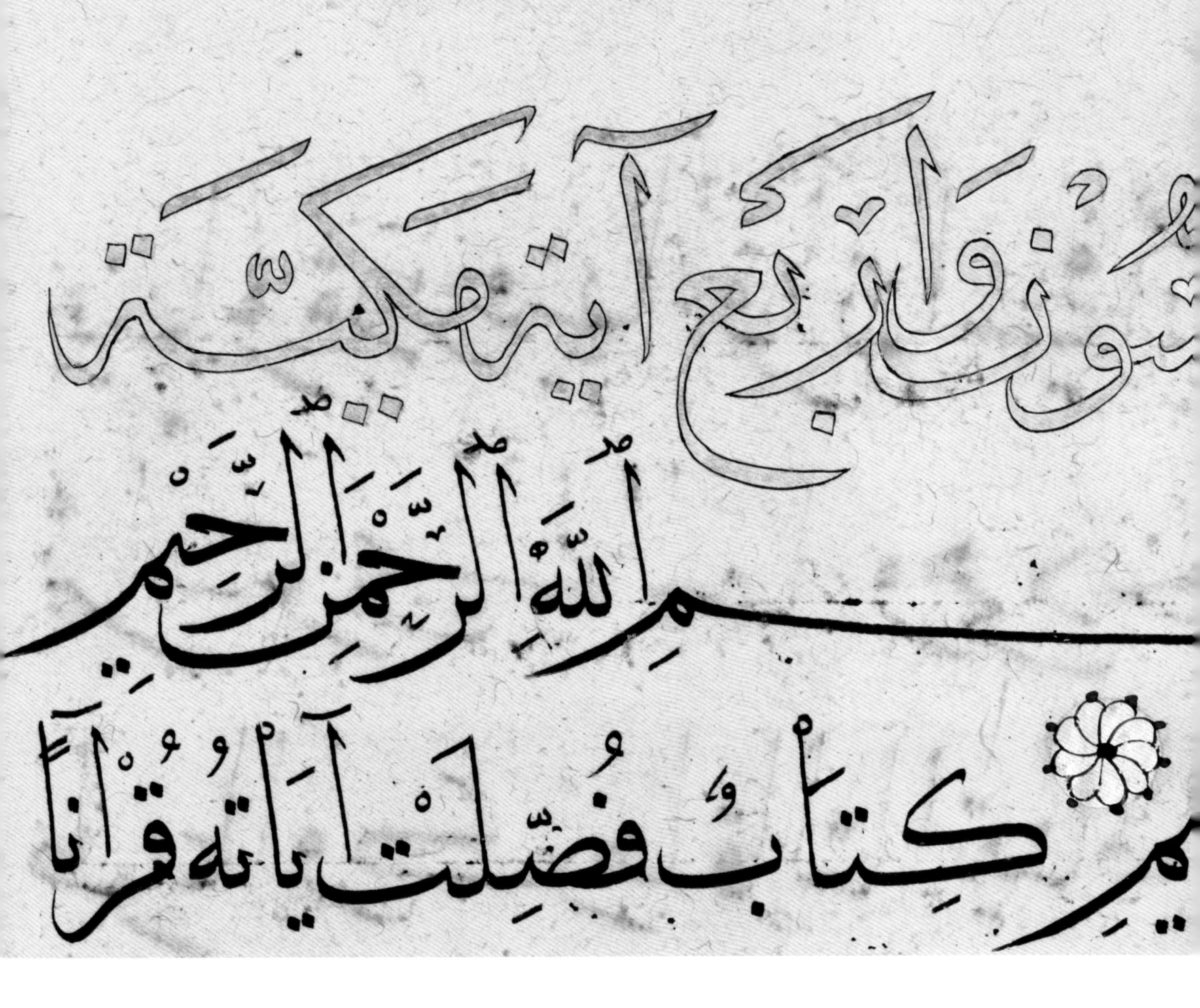

بسم الله الرحمن الرحيم

...م كتاب فصلت آياته قرآنا

سورة السجدة خمسون وأربع آية مكية

بسم الله الرحمن الرحيم

حم تنزيل من الرحمن الرحيم كتاب فصلت آياته قرآنا عربيا لقوم يعلمون بشيرا ونذيرا فأعرض أكثرهم فهم لا يسمعون وقالوا قلوبنا في أكنة مما تدعونا إليه وفي آذاننا وقر ومن بيننا وبينك حجاب فاعمل إننا عاملون قل إنما أنا بشر مثلكم يوحى إلي أنما إلهكم إله واحد فاستقيموا إليه واستغفروه وويل للمشركين الذين لا يؤتون الزكوة وهم بالآخرة هم كافرون إن الذين آمنوا وعملوا الصالحات لهم أجر غير ممنون قل أئنكم لتكفرون بالذي خلق الأرض في يومين وتجعلون له أندادا ذلك رب العالمين وجعل فيها رواسي من فوقها وبارك

عَلَىٰ مَكَانَتِكُمْ إِنِّي عَامِلٌ فَسَوْفَ تَعْلَمُونَ ۞ مَن يَأْتِيهِ عَذَابٌ يُخْزِيهِ وَيَحِلُّ عَلَيْهِ عَذَابٌ مُقِيمٌ ۞ إِنَّا أَنزَلْنَا عَلَيْكَ ٱلْكِتَابَ لِلنَّاسِ بِٱلْحَقِّ ۖ فَمَنِ ٱهْتَدَىٰ فَلِنَفْسِهِ ۖ وَمَن ضَلَّ فَإِنَّمَا يَضِلُّ عَلَيْهَا ۖ وَمَا أَنتَ عَلَيْهِم بِوَكِيلٍ ۞ ٱللَّهُ يَتَوَفَّى ٱلْأَنفُسَ حِينَ مَوْتِهَا وَٱلَّتِي لَمْ تَمُتْ فِي مَنَامِهَا ۖ فَيُمْسِكُ ٱلَّتِي قَضَىٰ عَلَيْهَا ٱلْمَوْتَ وَيُرْسِلُ ٱلْأُخْرَىٰ إِلَىٰ أَجَلٍ مُسَمًّى ۚ إِنَّ فِي ذَٰلِكَ لَآيَاتٍ لِّقَوْمٍ يَتَفَكَّرُونَ ۞ أَمِ ٱتَّخَذُوا مِن دُونِ ٱللَّهِ شُفَعَاءَ ۚ قُلْ أَوَلَوْ كَانُوا لَا يَمْلِكُونَ شَيْئًا وَلَا يَعْقِلُونَ ۞ قُل لِّلَّهِ ٱلشَّفَاعَةُ جَمِيعًا ۖ لَّهُ مُلْكُ ٱلسَّمَاوَاتِ وَٱلْأَرْضِ ۖ ثُمَّ إِلَيْهِ تُرْجَعُونَ ۞ وَإِذَا ذُكِرَ ٱللَّهُ وَحْدَهُ ٱشْمَأَزَّتْ قُلُوبُ ٱلَّذِينَ لَا يُؤْمِنُونَ بِٱلْآخِرَةِ ۖ وَإِذَا ذُكِرَ ٱلَّذِينَ مِن دُونِهِ إِذَا هُمْ يَسْتَبْشِرُونَ ۞ قُلِ ٱللَّهُمَّ فَاطِرَ ٱلسَّمَاوَاتِ

63
Leaf in *muhaqqaq* script
Probably Iran
14th century CE
Surah 79 (*al-Nazi'at*), v. 29 – Surah 80 (*'Abasa*), v. 11

Folio from an Arabic manuscript on paper, nine lines of black *muhaqqaq* script per page; interlinear Persian translation in small black *naskh* script; individual verses marked with gold rosettes pointed in blue and red; fifth verse divisions marked with gold marginal medallions between two gold diamonds containing the word *khamsa* (five) in gold Kufic script; tenth verse divisions marked with gold marginal roundels containing the word *'asharah* (ten) in gold Kufic script; *surah* headings in form of illuminated panel with title in white thulth in in gold cloud bands on a ground of darker gold with adjacent illuminated roundel in margin

47.5 × 30.2 cm

An unusual feature on this Qur'an leaf is the use of the Persian form of the final *kaf*, which was not typically used on Qur'anic manuscripts. Large-scale copies of the Qur'an in *muhaqqaq* script were popular in Iran and Egypt in the fourteenth century. It was not unusual for copies made in Iran or Anatolia to have interlinear Persian, or even Turkish, translations (see Safwat 1997, pp. 53, 91; Salameh 2001, no. 7; James 1992a, no. 10; James 1998, no. 54).

Two other leaves from the manuscript were sold at Christie's, 5 October 2010, lot 121.

64
Bifolium in *muhaqqaq* script
Iran or India
13th – 14th century CE
Surah 49 (*al-Hujurat*), v. 13 – Surah 50 (*Qaf*), v. 19

Bifolium from an Arabic manuscript on paper, eleven lines of bold *muhaqqaq* script per page; interlinear Persian translation in small red *naskh* script; individual verse divisions marked with gold rosettes; fifth verse divisions marked with tear-shaped medallions containing the word *khamsah* (five) reserved in gold Kufic on a blue ground; tenth verse division marked with marginal illuminated roundel with radiating finials

45 × 30 cm

This bifolium is chiefly remarkable for the magnificently illuminated *surah* heading, which stands in contrast to the rather ungainly *muhaqqaq* script. The script and the brittle, brown paper may indicate an Indian origin.

A section of the Qur'an is in the Chester Beatty Library, Dublin (Arberry 1967, no. 65, catalogued as Mamluk). Another leaf from the same manuscript was sold at Sotheby's, 12 October 2000, lot 40.

الى ربك منتهىها انما انت منذر من يخشىها
كانهم يوم يرونها لم يلبثوا الا عشية او
ضحىها

بسم الله الرحمن الرحيم

عبس وتولى ان جاءه الاعمى وما يدريك
لعله يزكى او يذكر فتنفعه الذكرى
اما من استغنى فانت له تصدى وما
عليك الا يزكى واما من جاءك يسعى وهو
يخشى فانت عنه تلهى كلا انها تذكرة

ذلك رجع بعيد ۞ قد علمنا ما تنقص
الارض منهم وعندنا كتاب حفيظ بل
كذبوا بالحق لما جاءهم فهم في امر مريج
افلم ينظروا الى السماء فوقهم كيف
بنيناها وزيناها وما لها من فروج
والارض مددناها والقينا فيها رواسى
وانبتنا فيها من كل زوج بهيج
تبصرة وذكرى لكل عبد منيب ونزلنا
من السماء ماء مباركا فانبتنا به جنات
وحب الحصيد والنخل باسقات لها طلع
نضيد رزقا للعباد واحيينا به

يؤمنون ز عليك إذا اسلموا قل لا تمنوا على
إسلامكم بل الله يمن عليكم إن هدا
كم للإيمان إن كنتم صادقين إن
الله يعلم غيب السموات والأرض
والله بصير بما تعملون

سورة ق والقرآن المجيد

بسم الله الرحمن الرحيم
ق والقرآن المجيد بل عجبوا أن
جاءهم منذر منهم فقال الكافرون
هذا شيء عجيب أإذا متنا وكنا ترابا

65
Bifolium in *muhaqqaq* script
Central Asia or Anatolia
14th century CE
Surah 81 (al-Takwir), v. 25 – Surah 82 (al-Infitar), v. 4

Bifolium from an Arabic manuscript on paper, three lines of black *muhaqqaq* script per page; interlinear Persian translation in black *naskh* script; individual verses marked with gold rosettes pointed in red and green; *surah* heading consisting of illuminated panel containing cartouche formed of two semicircles in which title and verse count are written in white *tawqi'* script, gold palmette outlined in blue extending into margin

28.5 × 18.6 cm

Though India was once believed to be the origin of these leaves from an unusual Qur'an (Losty 1982, p. 10; Geneva 1985, p. 143), Central Asia and Anatolia are now widely accepted as the more likely possibilities. Tim Stanley has argued that a Central Asian origin would account for certain archaic features such as the very narrow tall *muhaqqaq* script, reminiscent of pre-Ilkhanid Iranian Qur'ans (Stanley 1999, p. 22). Such features were also preserved in Chinese Qur'ans, which similarly remained removed from developments in Iran and the western Islamic lands. David James has suggested Anatolia on the basis of similarities with the illumination and script of two manuscripts almost certainly of Anatolian origin (James 1992a, p. 208).

Further leaves from the same manuscript are in, among other collections, the David Collection, Copenhagen (von Folsach 2001, no. 6), and the Chester Beatty Library, Dublin (Arberry 1967, no. 83). Leaves from the 6th *juz'* of the Qur'an have later, possibly Qajar, illuminated borders. For leaves of this type, see the leaf in the Nasser D. Khalili Collection (James 1992a, no. 51).

66
Bifolium in *muhaqqaq* script
Central Asia or Anatolia
14th century CE
Surah 78 (*al-Naba'*)

Bifolium from an Arabic manuscript on paper, three lines of black *muhaqqaq* script per page; interlinear Persian translation in black *naskh* script; individual verses marked with gold rosettes pointed in red and green

28.5 × 18.6 cm

This leaf comes from the same manuscript as no. 65.

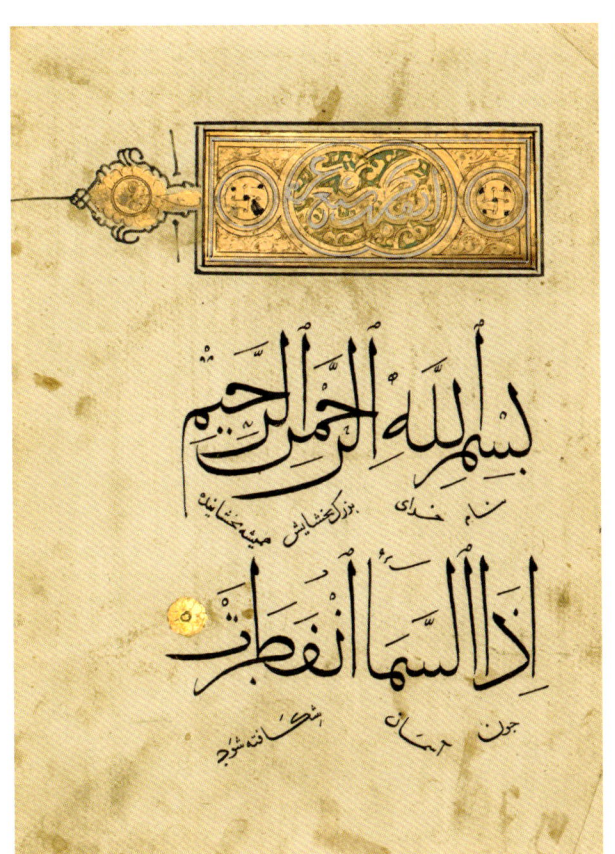

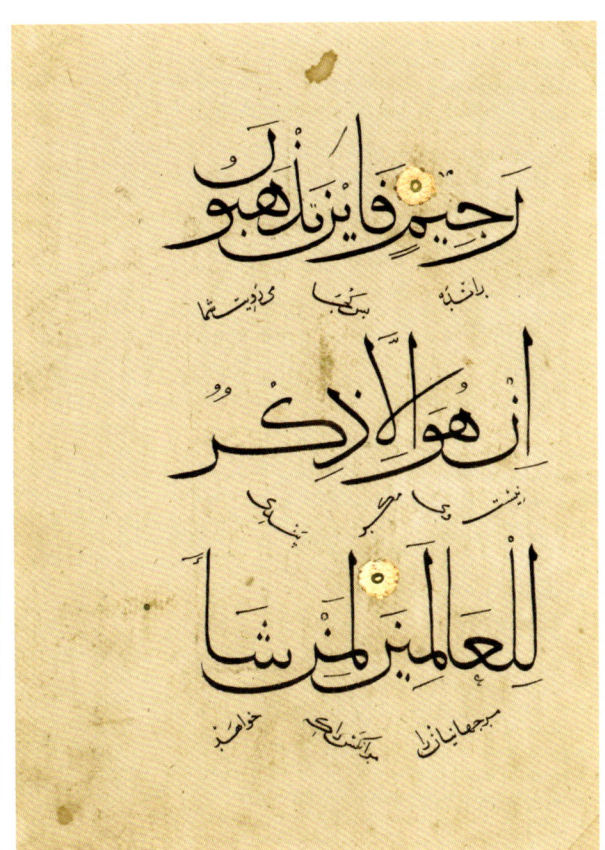

بسم الله الرحمن الرحيم
اذا السما انفطرت

رجيم فاين تذهبون
ان هو الا ذكر
للعالمين لمن شاء

ونهى النفس عن
الهوى فان الجنة
هى المأوى فسألناك

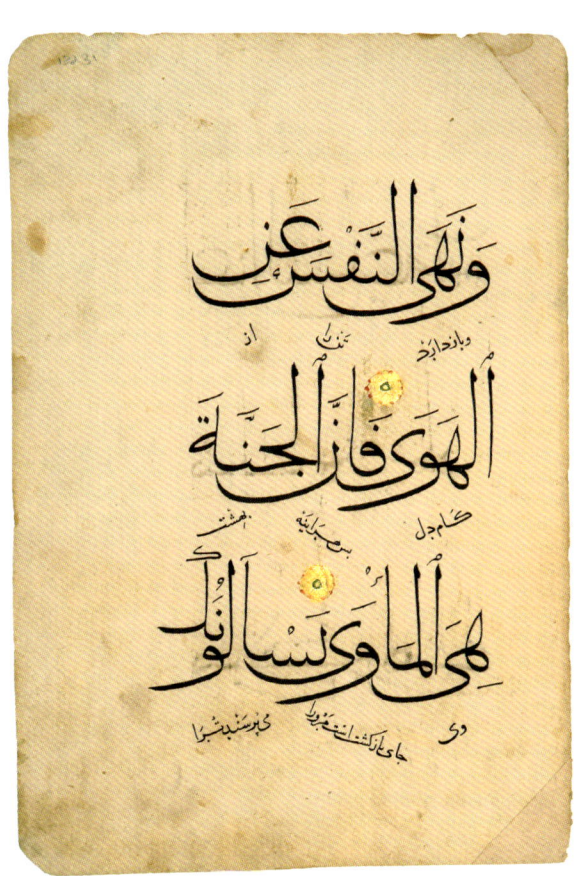

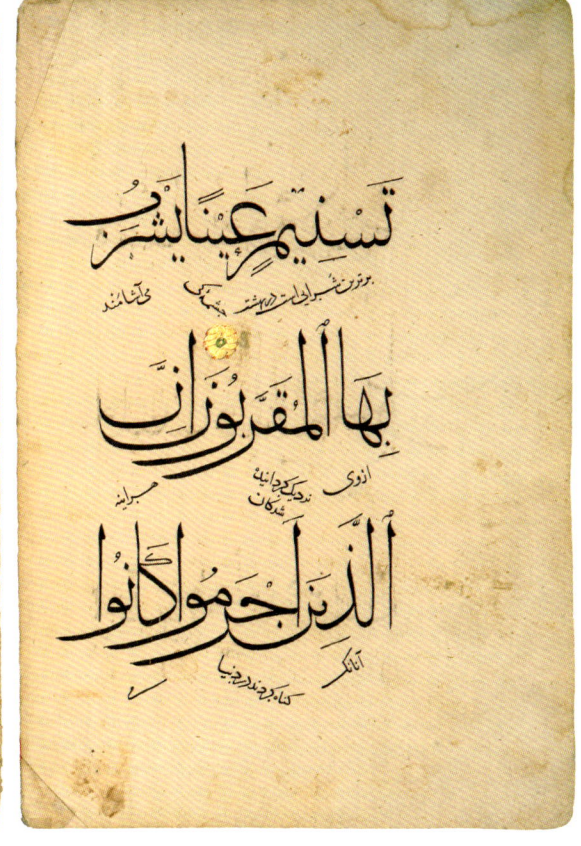

تسنيم عينا يشرب
بها المقربون
الذين جاهدوا فانوا

67
Leaf from a Qur'anic album
Probably Jala'irid Baghdad
c. 1370 CE
Surah 34 (*Saba'*), vv. 19–22

Folio from an Arabic manuscript on paper, five lines of black *muhaqqaq* script outlined in gold per page; text block ruled in gold, blue and red; individual verse divisions marked with roundels with illuminated gold central knot-motif and dotted border

43 × 35 cm

This leaf from a selection of Qur'anic verses is in a stately, monumental *muhaqqaq* script, carefully outlined in gold. Aboulala Soudavar has suggested on stylistic grounds that the manuscript was made in Baghdad for the Jala'irid ruler Shaykh Uways (Soudavar 1992, p. 50). While the style of illumination harks back to Ilkhanid imperial Qur'ans, the type of *muhaqqaq* script looks forward to the monumental Timurid script found on manuscripts such as the giant Qur'an traditionally ascribed to Baysunghur but now thought to have been made for Timur (see no. 69). The colophon of the manuscript, now in a private collection, gives the name of the scribe as 'Abu Muhammad 'Abd al-Qayyum ibn Muhammad ibn Karamshah-i Tabrizi'. Further leaves are in various museums and private collections. These include a leaf formerly in the Art and History Trust Collection, Washington D.C. (Soudavar 1992, no. 19); a further leaf in the David Collection, Copenhagen (von Folsach 2001, no. 8); a leaf exhibited in the Museum of Fine Arts, Houston (Roxburgh 2008, fig. 20), and two leaves exhibited in the Musée d'art et d'histoire, Geneva, in 1988 (James 1988, no. 23a-b).

فى شك من ربك على كل
شى حفيظ قل ادعوا الذ
ن زعمتم من دون الله لا يملكون
مثقال ذرة فى السموات
ولا فى الارض وما صم فيهما

68
Leaf in *muhaqqaq* script
Iran
c. 1370–1400 CE
Surah 2 (*al-Baqarah*), vv. 128–32

Folio from an Arabic manuscript on paper, five lines of black *muhaqqaq* script per page; text block framed with double gold and blue rules; vocalization and diacritics in black; *shaddah* and *tajwid* markings in red; individual verse devisions marked with polychrome and gold roundels of two alternating patterns; tenth verse division marked with large polychrome and gold oval medallion and small gold and polychrome roundel in margin

34.5 × 26.2 cm

This Qur'an leaf is in a beautiful, measured script. Guide lines, impressed on to the page to aid the scribe, are still clearly visible. The leaf is similar in format and aesthetic to no. 67, which is also written in five lines of *muhaqqaq* script within ruled borders, and is probably of a similar origin and date.

A very similar leaf also with clear guide lines, possibly from the same manuscript, is in the Nasser D. Khalili Collection (James 1992b, no. 35). David James has compared the illumination and script on that leaf to a thirty-volume Qur'an copied by a certain Shaykh Muhammad ibn Muhammad al-Tughra'i, known as Matarji, in 809 / 1406–07.

Another leaf from the same manuscript was exhibited in the Museum of Fine Arts, Houston, attributed to fifteenth-century Egypt or Syria (Roxburgh 2008, fig. 22).

وتب علينا انك انت التواب
الرحيم ربنا وابعث فيهم رسولا
منهم يتلوا عليهم اياتك ويعلمهم
الكتاب والحكمة و
يزكيهم انك انت العزيز الحكيم

69
Leaf in *bihari* script
North India
15th century CE
Surah 8 (*al-Anfal*), vv. 38–41

Folio from an Arabic manuscript on cream paper, fifteen lines of black *bihari* script per page; text block ruled in a double frame of red and blue; individual verses marked with gold roundels with dotted borders; large polychrome and gold tear-shaped marginal medallion marking beginning of tenth *juz'*; the word *allah* picked out in red; marginal text in red and black ink

52.6 × 31.4 cm

The unusually large size of this Qur'an in *bihari* script may indicate that it was produced for a mosque or a *madrasah*.

The term *bihari* is of obscure origin and is unlikely to refer to the Bihar region of India, where no tradition of manuscript copying and few great mosques or *madrasahs* existed (Losty 1982, p. 39).

The earliest dated Qur'an in *bihari* script, now in the Aga Khan Museum, was completed in 801 / 1399 in Gwalior, near Delhi (Canby 1998, no. 76). The tradition was relatively short, lasting only just over a century and dying out roughly at the same time as the consolidation of Mughal power in North India in the second quarter of the sixteenth century (see James 1992b, p. 104).

Bihari script is notable for the contrasting shapes of the vertical and horizontal letters, such as the thin line of the letter *alif* and the thick horizontal strokes of letters such as *nun* and *ta*. Although the origins of the script are obscure, it appears to have derived from the distinctive type of *naskh* script that evolved in India. The illumination, as is the case here, is typically bright and characterized by a palette of strong orange, red and blue (James 1992b, p. 102).

The outer margins contain a zigzag commentary on parts of the text, while the inner margin contains alternative readings for various words in red.

Two folios from the same Qur'an are in the Nasser D. Khalili Collection (James 1992b, no. 27).

تكون فتنة ويكون الدين كله
لله فان انتهوا فان الله بما
يعملون بصير وان تولوا فاعلموا
ان الله مولىكم نعم المولى ونعم النصير
واعلموا انما غنمتم من شيء فان لله
خمسه وللرسول ولذي القربى
واليتامى والمساكين وابن
السبيل ان كنتم آمنتم بالله وما
انزلنا على عبدنا يوم الفرقان
يوم التقى الجمعان والله على
كل شيء قدير اذ انتم
بالعدوة الدنيا وهم بالعدوة القصوى
والركب اسفل منكم ولو تواعدتم
لاختلفتم في الميعاد ولكن
ليقضي الله امرا كان مفعولا

70
Line from the Baysunghur Qur'an
Probably Samarkand
c. 1400 CE
Surah 49 (*al-Hujarat*), part of v. 12

Line from an Arabic manuscript on buff paper in dark brown *muhaqqaq* script; vocalization and diacritics in dark brown; *tajwid* markings in red

18.5 × 94.7 cm

This large fragment comes from a magnificent Qur'an of extraordinary dimensions, traditionally ascribed to Baysunghur (1397–1434 CE), the grandson of Timur. Scholarship now largely agrees that it is the giant Qur'an made for Timur mentioned in Qadi Ahmad's sixteenth-century treatise on calligraphy (Soudavar 1992, p. 59). The great marble Qur'an stand commissioned by Ulugh Beg after Timur's death in 1405, originally located in the great chamber of the Friday Mosque in Samarkand, is thought to have been made specifically for this Qur'an (Lentz and Lowry 1989, p. 36).

Surviving complete pages from the manuscript measure a giant *c.* 177 × 110 cm, and it has been estimated that the complete manuscript would have consisted of around 800 bifolia (James 1992b, p. 18). Qadi Ahmad mentions that a folio from the manuscript was in the possession of Mawlana Malik, who is probably the calligrapher Malik al-Daylami, indicating that the manuscript had already been partially split up by the sixteenth century (Soudavar 1992, p. 59). According to various sources, the manuscript was taken from Samarkand during Nadir Shah's occupation of the city in 1740. Part of the manuscript was placed in the *imamzadah* of Shahzadah Ibrahim ibn 'Ali ibn Musa al-Rida' by a local ruler who had participated in Nadir Shah's campaign.

The first reference to Baysunghur in connection with the Qur'an goes back to the collector of Oriental manuscripts James Baillie Fraser, who saw the section in Quchan in north-east Iran (James 1992b, p. 21).

Other pages and lines from the manuscript are now in the Astan-i Quds Library, Mashhad; the Gulistan Library, Tehran; the Malik Library, Tehran; the Museum of Ancient Iran, Tehran; the National Library of Iran, Tehran; the Reza 'Abbasi Museum, Tehran; the Nasser D. Khalili Collection; the Metropolitan Museum, New York; The Art and History Trust Collection, Washington D.C.; the David Collection, Copenhagen; and numerous private collections (for a fuller list see James 1992b, p. 22).

Pages and fragments have also appeared in numerous auction sales. These include a whole page as well as a fragment of three lines with a *surah* heading that appeared at Sotheby's, 10 October 1998, lots 168, 169. A number of replacement pages are known, probably made for missing sections in Iran in the eighteenth or nineteenth century (James 1992b, no. 3).

ن الـ

امنوا اجتنبوا كث

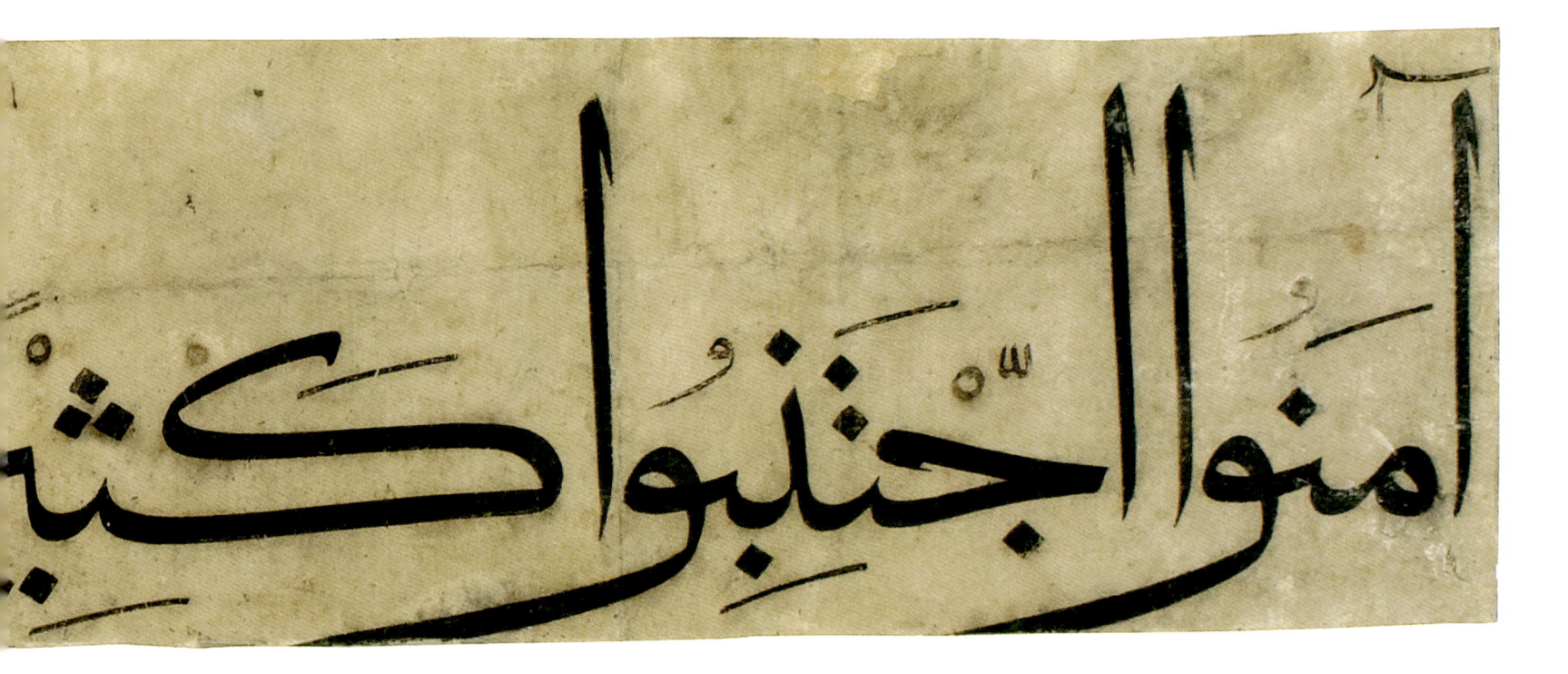

برا من الظن ان بعض

71
Leaf in *bihari* script
North India
15th century CE
Surah 42 *(al-Shura)*, vv. 27–36

Folio from an Arabic manuscript on paper, thirteen lines of *bihari* script in alternating blue, black and gold ink per page; text block within a single gold frame; large polychrome and gold tear-shaped marginal medallion marking a quarter *juz'*; marginal commentary on both sides; page trimmed at the border, cut to fit around medallion

22.5 × 21.3 cm

Like no. 69, this is a leaf from a brightly illuminated fifteenth-century Qur'an in *bihari* script.

A large part of the manuscript from which this leaf comes is in Saudi Arabia (Riyadh 1986, no. 90). Further pages are in the Los Angeles County Museum of Art (Pal 1993, no. 40), the Metropolitan Museum of Art, New York, and the David Collection, Copenhagen (von Folsach 2001, no. 14).

بقدر ما يشاء انه بعباده خبير
بصير وهو الذي ينزل
الغيث من بعد ما قنطوا
وينشر رحمته وهو الولي
الحميد ومن آياته خلق
السموات والأرض وما
بث فيهما من دابة وهو
على جمعهم اذا يشاء قدير
وما أصابكم من مصيبة
فبما كسبت أيديكم ويعفو
عن كثير وما أنتم
بمعجزين في الأرض
وما لكم من دون الله

72
Leaf in *muhaqqaq* and *naskh* script
Ottoman Empire
c. 1500 CE
Surah 9 (*al-Tawbah*), vv. 83–95

Arabic manuscript on thick burnished paper, thirteen lines per page, three lines of large *muhaqqaq* script at the top, centre and bottom with five lines of small *naskh* script in between; vocalization and diacritics in black, *tajwid* markers in form of small red letters; text block set in gold and blue frame; individual verse divisions marked with blue roundels with red dots around the edge

42.4 × 29.4 cm

Qur'ans in combinations of scripts in varying sizes were made in Iran and the Ottoman Empire in the fifteenth and sixteenth centuries (James 1992b, nos. 7, 8, 19, 35, 36, 40, 43, 44, 46, 48). This Qur'an is in a classic combination of three lines of large *muhaqqaq* alternating with multiple lines of small *naskh*. The glossy paper and the rather simply executed blue roundels are probably indicative of an Ottoman origin.

أنى يؤفكون ۞ اتخذوا الأحبار

ورهبانهم أرباباً من دون الله والمسيح ابن مريم وما أمروا الا
ليعبدوا إلها واحدا لا إله إلا هو سبحانه عما يشركون ۞ يريدون
أن يطفئوا نور الله بأفواههم ويأبى الله إلا أن يتم نوره ولو كره
الكافرون ۞ هو الذي أرسل رسوله بالهدى ودين الحق
ليظهره على الدين كله ولو كره المشركون ۞ يا أيها الذين

آمنوا إن كثيرا من الأحبار والرهبان

ليأكلون أموال الناس بالباطل ويصدون عن سبيل الله
والذين يكنزون الذهب والفضة ولا ينفقونها في سبيل الله
فبشرهم بعذاب أليم ۞ يوم يحمى عليها في نار جهنم فتكوى
بها جباههم وجنوبهم وظهورهم هذا ما كنزتم لأنفسكم
فذوقوا ما كنتم تكنزون ۞ إن عدة الشهور عند الله اثنا

عشر شهرا في كتاب الله يوم خلق

73
Leaf in gold and black *muhaqqaq* script
Iran
Mid 16th century CE
Surah 68 (*al-Qalam*), v. 32 – Surah 69 (*al-Haqqah*)

Folio from an Arabic manuscript on paper, ten and twelve lines of alternating gold and black *muhaqqaq* script per page, each line set within ruled and shaded panel; text block ruled in gold, blue, green and orange; individual verse divisions marked with gold rosettes pointed in blue; fifth verse divisions marked with blue marginal palmettes bordered in gold filled with gold trefoil and polychrome floral scroll; tenth verse divisions marked with gold marginal octagonal stars bordered in blue filled with polychrome floral scroll; *hizb* division marked in margin in gold *thulth* script; *surah* heading in white *thulth* in gold cartouche set within gold and blue illuminated panel

40.2 × 29 cm

The manuscript from which this leaf comes is a very early example of a Qur'an where the text is set within coloured panels, a format that does not seem to have become popular until the eighteenth century. The script and illumination on this leaf are otherwise typical of mid sixteenth-century Safavid Qur'ans (see e.g. von Folsach 2001, no. 13; Istanbul 2010, nos. 74–76).

Other leaves from this manuscript are in the Nasser D. Khalili Collection (James 1992b, no. 42) and a private collection in Geneva. Several further leaves have been sold at Sotheby's, including two leaves on 30 April 2010, lot 6.

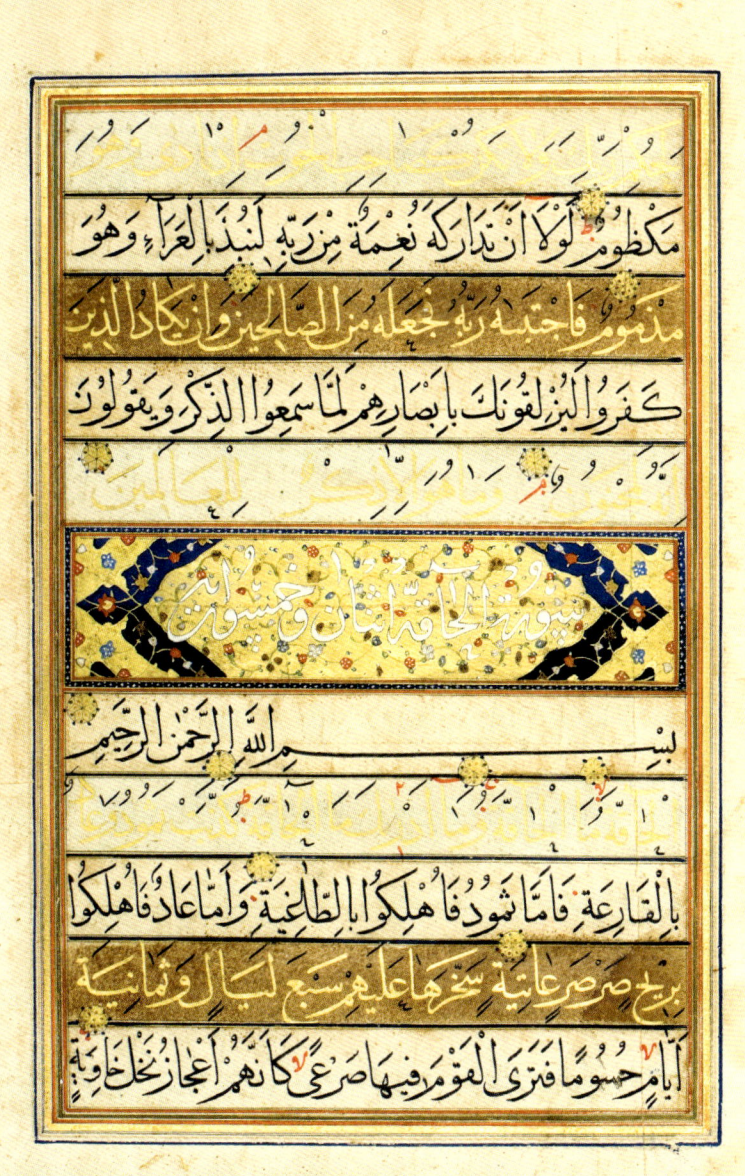

مكظوم لولا ان تداركه نعمة من ربه لنبذ بالعرا وهو
مذموم فاجتباه ربه فجعله من الصالحين وان يكاد الذين
كفروا ليزلقونك بابصارهم لما سمعوا الذكر ويقولون
انه لمجنون وما هو الا ذكر للعالمين

سورة الحاقة ثمان وخمسون آية

بسم الله الرحمن الرحيم

الحاقة ما الحاقة وما ادراك ما الحاقة كذبت ثمود وعاد
بالقارعة فاما ثمود فاهلكوا بالطاغية واما عاد فاهلكوا
بريح صرصر عاتية سخرها عليهم سبع ليال وثمانية
ايام حسوما فترى القوم فيها صرعى كانهم اعجاز نخل خاوية

Bibliography

Abu Dhabi 2007
The Arts of Islam: Treasures from the Nasser D Khalili Collection, exhibition catalogue, Abu Dhabi, 2007

Amsterdam 1999
Earthly Beauty, Heavenly Art: Art of Islam, exhibition catalogue, Amsterdam, 1999

Arberry 1967
A.J. Arberry, *The Koran Illuminated,* Dublin, 1967

Bahrain 1996
Beit al-Qur'an, Bahrain, 1996

Blair 2006
Sheila S. Blair, *Islamic Calligraphy,* Edinburgh, 2006

Blair and Bloom 2006
Sheila S. Blair and Jonathan M. Bloom, *Cosmophilia: Islamic Art from the David Collection,* Boston, Mass., 2006

Bloom 2001
Jonathan M. Bloom, *Paper Before Print: The History and Impact of Paper in the Islamic World,* New Haven, 2001

Bloom 1989
Jonathan M. Bloom, 'The Blue Koran. An early Fatimid Kufic manuscript from the Maghrib', in François Déroche (ed.), *Les Manuscrits du Moyen-Orient. Essais de codicologie et de paléographie,* Istanbul and Paris, 1989, pp. 95–99

von Bothmer 1987
H.C. Graf von Bothmer, 'Arkitekturbilder im Koran. Eine Prachthandschrift der Umayyadenzeit aus dem Yemen', *Pantheon,* XLV, Munich, 1987

von Bothmer 1997
H.C. Graf von Bothmer, 'Die Buchkunst des Islams', *Orientalis che Buchkunst in Gotha: Ausstellung zum 350jährigen Jubiläum der Forschungs-und Landesbibliothek Gotha,* Gotha, 1997

Canby 1998
Sheila Canby, *Princes, Poets and Paladins: Islamic and Indian paintings from the collection of Prince and Princess Sudruddin Aga Khan,* London, 1998

Déroche 1983
François Déroche, *Catalogue des manuscrits arabes. Deuxième partie : Manuscrits musulmans. Tome I, Les manuscrits du Coran,* Paris, 1983

Déroche 1992
François Déroche, *The Abbasid Tradition: Qur'ans of the 8th to the 10th Centuries AD,* Oxford, 1992

Déroche 1999
François Déroche, 'Note sur les fragments coraniques anciens de Katta Langar (Ouzbékistan)', *Cahiers d'Asie centrale,* no. 7, Paris, 1999

Déroche & von Gladiss 1999
François Déroche and Almut von Gladiss, *Buchkunst zur Ehre Allahs: Der Prachtkoran im Museum für Islamische Kunst,* Berlin, 1999

Dodge 1970
Bayard Dodge, *The Fihrist of al-Nadim: A Tenth-Century Survey of Muslim Culture,* 2 vols., New York, 1970

Doha 2006
Languages of the Pen, exhibition catalogue, Doha, 2006

Doha 2008
Museum of Islamic Art, Doha, Qatar, exhibition catalogue, Doha, 2008

Duda 1992
Dorothea Duda, *Die Illuminierten Handschriften und Inkunabeln der Österreichischen Nationalbibliothek, Band 5, Teil 1: Islamische Handschriften* Vienna, 1992

Dutton 2000
Yasin Dutton, 'Red dots, green dots, yellow dots and blue: Some reflections on the vocalisation of early Qur'anic manuscripts', Part I, *Journal of Qur'anic Studies,* no. 1, London, 2000

Ettinghausen *et al.* 2001
R. Ettinghausen, O. Grabar and M. Jenkins-Madina, *Islamic Art and Architecture, 650–1250,* New Haven, 2001

von Folsach 2001
Kjeld von Folsach, *Art from the World of Islam in the David Collection,* Copenhagen, 2001

Fraser and Kwiatkowski 2006
Marcus Fraser and Will Kwiatkowski, *Ink and Gold: Islamic Calligraphy,* London, 2006

Geneva 1985
Treasures of Islam, exhibition catalogue, Geneva, 1985

George 2010
Alain George, *The Rise of Islamic Calligraphy,* London, 2010

Gruendler 1993
> 'The Development of the Arabic Scripts: From the Nabatean Era to the First Islamic Century. *Harvard Semitic Studies*, 43, 1993

Istanbul 2010a
> *The 1400th Anniversary of the Qur'an*, exhibition catalogue, Istanbul, 2010

Istanbul 2010b
> *Treasures of the Aga Khan Museum*, exhibition catalogue, Istanbul, 2010

James 1980
> David James, *Qur'ans and Bindings from the Chester Beatty Library*, London, 1980

James 1988
> David James, *Islamic Calligraphy*, Geneva, 1988

James 1992b
> David James, *After Timur: Qur'ans of the 15th and 16th centuries*, London, 1992

James 1992a
> David James, *The Master Scribes: Qur'ans of the 10th to 14th centuries AD*, London, 1992

Kühnel 1972
> Ernst Kühnel, *Islamische Schriftkunst*, Graz, 1972

Lings 1976
> Martin Lings, *The Qur'anic Art of Calligraphy and Illumination*, London, 1976

Lings and Safadi 1976
> Martin Lings and Yasin Safadi, *The Qur'an – Catalogue of an Exhibition of Qur'an Manuscripts at the British Library*, exhibition catalogue, London, 1976

London 2004
> *Heaven on Earth: Art from Islamic Lands*, exhibition catalogue, London, 2004

Losty 1982
> J.P. Losty, *The Art of the Book in India,* London, 1982

Mainz am Rhein 2001
> *Museum für Islamische Kunst. Staatliche Museen zu Berlin, Preußischer Kulturbesitz*, Mainz am Rhein, 2001

al-Munajjid 1960
> Salahuddin al-Munajjid, *Al-Kitab al-'arabi al-makhtut ila'l-qarn al-'ashir al-hijri*, Cairo, 1960

New York 1992
> *Al-Andalus*, exhibition catalogue, New York, 1992

O'Kane 1996
> Bernard O'Kane, 'Monumentality in Mamluk and Mongol Art and Architecture,' *Art History* , vol. 19, no. 4, 1996, pp. 499–522

Pal 1993
> Pratapaditya Pal, *Indian Painting: A Catalogue of the Los Angeles County Museum of Art Collection*, Los Angeles, 1993

Paris 1982
> *De Carthage à Kairouan – 2000 ans d'art et d'histoire en Tunisie*, exhibition catalogue, Paris, 1982

Paris 1999
> *Maroc. Les trésors du royaume*, exhibition catalogue, Paris, 1999

Paris 2001
> *L'Art du livre arabe*, exhibition catalogue, Paris, 2001

Paris 2007
> *Chefs d'œuvre islamiques de l'Aga Khan Museum*, exhibition catalogue, Paris, 2007

Rice 1955
> D.S. Rice, *The Unique Ibn al-Bawwab Manuscript in the Chester Beatty Library*, Dublin, 1955

Riyadh 1985
> *Unity in Islamic Art*, exhibition catalogue, Riyadh, 1985

Riyadh 1986
> *Arabic Calligraphy in Manuscripts*, exhibition catalogue, Riyadh, 1986

Roxburgh 2008
> David J. Roxburgh, *Writing the Word of God: Calligraphy and the Qur'an*, Houston, 2008

Safadi 1978
> Yasin Safadi, *Islamic Calligraphy,* London, 1978

Saint Laurent 1989
> Beatrice Saint Laurent, 'The Identification of a Magnificent Koran Manuscript', in *Manuscrits du moyen- orient: essais de codicologie et paléographie*, in François Déroche (ed.), *Les Manuscrits du Moyen-Orient. Essais de codicologie et de paléographie*, Istanbul and Paris, 1989, pp. 115–24

Safwat 1997
> Nabil Safwat. *The Harmony of Letters: Islamic Calligraphy from the Tareq Rajab Museum*, Singapore, 1997

Salameh 2001
> Khader Salameh, *The Qur'an Manuscripts in the al-Haram al-Sharif Islamic Museum, Jerusalem*, Reading, 2001

Shebunin 1891
> A.F Shebunin, 'Kuficheskij Koran imperatorskoj Sankt-Petersburgsko publichnoj biblioteki', in *Zapiski Vostochnogo Otdelenija imperatorskogo russkogo arkheologicheskogo obshchestva*, vol. 6, 1891, pp. 69–133

Soudavar 1992
> A. Soudavar, *Art of the Persian Courts: Selections from the Art and History Trust Collection*, New York, 1992

Stanley 1995
> Tim Stanley, *The Qur'an and Calligraphy. A Selection of Fine Manuscript Material. Bernard Quaritch, catalogue 1213*, London, 1995

Stanley 1999
> Tim Stanley, *The Qur'an, Scholarship and the Islamic Arts of the Book,* Bernard Quaritch Ltd., London, 1999

Uspenskij and Pisarev 1905
> F.I. Uspenskij and S.I. Pisarev, *Samarkandskij kuficheskii Koran po predaniju tret'im khalifom Osmanom (644–656)*, St Petersburg, 1905

Welch 1979
> Anthony Welch, *Calligraphy in the Arts of the Muslim World*, Folkestone, 1979

Wright 2009
> Elaine Wright, *Islam: Faith, Art, Culture. Manuscripts of the Chester Beatty Library*, London, 2009